MY LIfE BEFORE AND AFTER CHRIST INCLUDING SERVICE UNTO GOD

AND

JESUS IS COMING AGAIN

SOON!!!!!

BY

CHARLES A. DE LAND
(CHUCK)

ISBN: 0-75961-514-4

This book is printed on acid free paper.

1stBooks - rev. 03/16/01

MY LIFE BEFORE AND AFTER CHRIST

Charles (Chuck) A. De Land

HE WALKED

Have I ever told you about Jesus
How He came to earth to die
To hang on a cross at Calvary
For the sins of you and I

He walked on earth without a sin
To show us how to victory win
Love your God with all your heart
His love for you will never depart

Trod here in this land of dying
On His Fathers love He was relying
Then He went into the earth
To give we sinners a new birth

All because He loves each one
Then when His earthly work was done
Went to heaven to His throne
To welcome His own to their new home

Charles (Chuck) A. De Land

THE EARLY YEARS

For fifty five plus years of my life I wandered around this world looking for something better than I had and not knowing what it was I wanted. I don't mean by this that I never thought about God or hell, or salvation, I just mean these things were only fleeting thoughts at best.

I remember never being able to please, no matter what I did or said. If my report cards from school showed B and C, they should have been A and B, or better still all A. If I found a job on Saturday and earned some money I should have let my brother have the job, so as long as I didn't give him the job I had to give him half of the money from the job.

After awhile I got tired of trying to do anything right, so I quit trying and took all of the abuse that went along with it, including whippings when I was younger, I quit trying to achieve good grades in school as well and as a result had to take some grades over, so this made me older than most of my class mates.

With this kind of a background it is easy to understand why I began to be a very defensive person, and fighting was the easiest way to be defensive, so I fell into this way of self defense. This led into more trouble at home, and as a result of these fights the law was laid down that I would never be the one to start a fight, and if I did hold myself in check until someone else took the first swing I could fight back. If I didn't hold my temper and swung first I got whipped for it. Then if I didn't swing first and got beat in the fight I got whipped when I came home, needless to say after a few whippings for losing fights I got good, even better than good, I found out that if I worked things right it was easy to antagonize the other guy to the point where he would lose his head and swing first, then it was my turn to beat up someone in a

4

legal fashion, as far as my dads rules were concerned, and I took full advantage of that situation.

This soon brought me more, and bigger problems, because even though the other guy took the first swing at me I shouldn't be beating them up so bad, even if I was smaller and lighter than they were, the police frown on such things, and so do his parents. This led me into other difficulties as you will see.

I became a loner, never caring if I was with some one or not. If I wasn't with someone I didn't need to worry about fights, or other kinds of trouble, and this aloneness fed on itself and I learned not to communicate with others in any manner. My own separate dream world took me into many places and experiences where I didn't get into trouble as long as I didn't act on them.

Then we moved into the city, and of all things another brother was born, my brothers were the biggest cause for my actions as it was, and now another one to make my life miserable. But there was a girl who lived across the street who saw something in me that needed tenderness, so she showed me compassion, and tenderness, and started pulling me out of the shell I had taken myself into.

But this didn't last long because in the space of a year and a half we moved three times, went to two different schools, then moving to another small town where I spent the rest of my growing up years. During my stay in the other neighborhoods in the city I only partially got into trouble, usually when I would start to I would think of Emogene, and how she had helped me to stay straight for a while, then before long rebellion would set in again, and then it was just forget her and go headlong into whatever it was I wanted to pursue.

In the first neighborhood there was a refrigerated warehouse where some meat packing companies stored and distributed their wares to retail grocers in the city. These were carried in refrigerated trucks that returned to the warehouse about four o'clock, were plugged into the special electrical outlets which ran the refrigeration units on the truck. With this unit operating the trucks had to be loaded, and then locked up for the night. Each driver gave his order to the kid boss, who just happened to be the toughest kid there, so after working my way into the gang, it took me three days to go from starting to the top job, I was really well established and the job was a good one that paid $1.50 a day for me, and fifty cents for each of the other kids. If they didn't work fast enough they got their pay reduced, and I got the extra, which was a good arrangement for me.

However this only lasted about five months and we moved again. Here the jobs were scarce and the pay much less, setting up displays in front of a hardware, sweeping it, a drug store, and a grocery store, which were all in the same complex. Then I hauled out the trash and burned it. I still had to share with big brother, without his helping me, but I just did it and let it go at that.

I also had a chance to work on the safety patrol at school, and I guess this was what gave me the idea I could get ahead without having to be such a tough guy, and I moved up to being the Captain for our school, and was really proud that I had made it there without having to fight anyone for the honor. I also found out I could hit a baseball pretty good, so I made the school team as catcher, and the only left handed batter in the grade school league, which was a great break for me as the other teams didn't know how to pitch to a lefty. They either threw fast straight balls, or slow curves, or out of fear of hitting me they would walk me, so my batting average was pretty good.

This too was short lived as we made our move from the city, out to a small country village, about twenty five miles from the city, and that's where I finished growing up. In many ways small towns are not much different than cities, you still have to fight to prove yourself, and if you lose you go down in standings. Needless to say I had learned my lessons well, and I wouldn't pick, or start a fight, this caused the others to think I was a coward, so they would take the first swing, and miss, then just so no one could say I had started the fight, I had learned to let them have the second swing, which also missed, then they were all mine, and I had a ball taking them apart.

After the first four tried it at least once, and some of them twice, it was decided I was the boss in our age group, and the two groups older than us, which took in the fifth through the eighth grades, so whatever I did went a long way in or out of school.

By the time I got into the ninth grade it was a standing joke in town that our house was commonly known in the police circles as post thirteen, and my parents could never quite figure out why. We were always in bed by nine, or nine thirty, and yet there would be reports of my brother and myself being around town as late as eleven, or on some occasions twelve midnight. To the best of my knowledge our parents never knew until we were well into our thirties, that we went out of my bedroom window, slid down the post of the side porch, and set out for whatever adventure was planned for that night.

On several occasions I can recall the lights coming on and finding Mom, or Dad, or both, along with one or two police officers telling us to get out of bed so they could see if we were undressed, or if the bed was warm enough to indicate we had been there for some time, or had just jumped in, in time to close our eyes and pretend we were asleep. We were usually able to put on a good enough act that they couldn't be sure if we had just gotten in, or had been there and sleeping when they came up after us.

From about fourteen years old, until I was sixteen, I and various other boys ran away from home many times, and it got so bad that no one in town was allowed to go with me, or even be seen talking to me, so I went to work on farms around the community, earning at least a dollar a day, and room and board, this worked good for the summers, but after the harvest there was no work, so I finally quit school and went to live with my sister and her husband.

THE NAVY EXPERIENCE

It didn't take long and I was back into my old habits, and picked up with some guys who were the same as I was, and tired of being broke all of the time besides, so we got into some real troubles, like gaining access to some small businesses and walking off with whatever we could find to convert into ready cash. The law finally caught up with one of the guys, and he was given the choice of enlisting in the Armed Forces, (W. W. 2 was in it's infancy then), or being jailed for his crimes. Needless to say he went into the Army to avoid the jail sentence. After the second one got caught and received the same sentence, I decided I didn't want to be number three, and since I hadn't been identified by them as yet I enlisted in the Navy while I was still sixteen, I changed my birth certificate, was accepted and shipped to Great Lakes for training in Boot Camp.

This was a way to get a new start and give up my old ways of fighting, and being in all kinds of trouble all of the time, the only problem with that line of thinking was, my brain didn't seem able to wipe out all of the earlier years and their problems. For example, I was sitting on my bunk, the fourth one up, when a guy came in with stripes going from his wrist to his elbow, and said fall out into formation and get ready for complete physical, shots, and be sworn into the Navy. My reply was sez who, his was sez I, and make it on the double.

I didn't know at that time he was a Chief Petty Officer, and those stripes told of his years in the Navy, I figured I wasn't sworn in yet and I wasn't going to be taking orders from some one who just comes in and says move, so I came down off that top bunk, landed on my toes, and came up to take a swing at him. The only trouble with that was some one had tried that same thing on him before, and as I came up my fist headed for his chin, it missed because, it was deflected by his arm, and his fist headed for my chin didn't miss, mostly because I never saw it coming, all the way from the floor up. Then when I woke up a pail of water had been poured over me to help me regain my composure, and when he explained to me I must have slipped and knocked myself out, I readily agreed and ran out to get into formation as I had originally been ordered to do.

That was just the first day of twelve weeks of Boot Camp training, and the days were much like the first, except I didn't come out of my bunk swinging at people. Up and to chow at six thirty, drill grinder at eight, chow at twelve, then specialized training, (rifle range, bayonet practice, boxing, physical education, and etc.) started at one thirty. Chow again at six, then free time for washing clothes, showers, and shoe shining, with lights out at ten sharp.

With Boot Camp over I headed for California, and wound up as a Seaman Guard, in of all places, the Brig, at Camp Shoemaker. Can't you just see me guarding prisoners? I may not have been a big time outlaw before I got into this mans Navy, but I still couldn't really see me guarding prisoners. Then I found out I was to be on inside guard duty, and again I couldn't believe my ears when the Duty Officer said, go on solitary confinement duty in building twenty. It turns out this was a square building, thirty six by thirty six feet square, with four inner rooms, each one six by six feet in the center of the building with a passage around the outside of these rooms, or cells as they were in all truth. There was one exterior door in the building, in each cell was a stool, a wash basin, a bunk, and once every two weeks the prisoners were allowed a shower.

This too soon became routine, and I learned to smoke, (or rather I learned to hold a lighted cigarette), between my fingers, the coals a given distance from my fingers to give a built in timer for five, six, or seven minute intervals, before it got hot on my fingers and woke me up so I could make my verbal reports every ten minutes to the outside officer on duty.

I had applied for submarine school when I was in Boot Camp, and found out after I had been in Shoemaker about three months that I couldn't make it because my teeth weren't good enough, so I applied for overseas duty. It didn't take long and I was on my way to the Southwest Pacific theatre of operation.

I arrived in New Zeeland, and was assigned to the 38th C.B. Battalion and moved immediately to New Hebrides, to build three ship berthing docks so that supplies could be brought in and off loaded. No sooner was this assignment completed than five other men and myself, who had come over together from Shoemaker, were detached and assigned to the Second Marine Division, and headed for Guadalcanal and the invasion there.

This invasion was a bitter struggle for survival and victory, with each skirmish a major battle, as we saw them through our eyes. After a lot of advances, holds, and advances we were able to secure much of the island. Then soon after a resting period, and a chance to relax for a couple of weeks, we six were detached and reassigned.

At least this time we went to a Navy Unit. It was called Navy Advanced Base Unit-10, or NABU-10 for short. Our objective was to put military personnel ashore by waves, with us as our name would indicate the number one wave, then number three, and then we went into the supply waves, five, six, and as many others as were required to get all supplies ashore for the conclusion to the securing of the island. Then after some more island hopping we landed at New Guinea, and put several waves ashore, then after we had pulled out of there we returned to Guadalcanal for reorganization, and another group of islands to invade. This time they were called the Admiralty Islands, I don't know where the name came from but I guess that is not important.

When I hit the beach there in the first wave it turned out to be one of those places you hope you never see or hear of again. The Japanese were well secured from the first line right back up into the hills surrounding the bay. They had their cannons in the hills, their mortars at the base of the hills, and their machine guns, and twenty M.M. guns from the base of those hills all the way out to the waters edge. As we came in they were ready, and waited until we were in point blank range and then opened up with every piece they had.

Landing craft were flying out of the water like chips of wood, with bodies doing the same thing, while the screams of those who were hit pierced the air louder than the projectiles which were flying around us, the water was churning with bullets, and most of it was red from the blood of those who could no longer scream. After sever hours of bitter combat a beachhead was secured, we were out of ammunition for our own guns, and almost out of fuel from the third wave, when we were ordered to return to the mother ship immediately.

When we arrived along side for refueling and replenishing our ammunition, I was ordered to the fantail to tie up at the starboard yard arm and report immediately. Not knowing what was going on I pulled back to the fantail in a hurry and after securing there climbed the Jacobs Ladder to the main deck and reported to the quarterdeck. When the Duty Officer saw me he ordered me to report to the Captains Quarters on the double. In an even greater state of perplexity I headed for the Captains Cabin.

When I knocked, and was ordered in, I was wondering what I had done to foul up bad enough for the Captain to have to be the one to straighten me out. I flipped him a highball, came to attention and waited for whatever it was he had called me in for, when he said at ease, eyes right, my eyes nearly fell out into my cheekbones when they focused on a man standing there whom I had met only a few times, under casual circumstances.

He was wearing the stripes of a full Commander, and still didn't look to me as if he had enough brains to come in out of the rain. You see I had gone with his sister for a while when I was stationed at Shoemaker, and had met him through her. Before I had joined up I had been a telephone operator in our small town on the all night shift. One night one of the local service men called home and I had a chance to talk with the operator from San Hose, California, and we made it a point to call each other every night after that, and so when I went to California it was only natural that I would contact her, when I did we started dating.

It was nothing serious, just a service man a long way from home and lonely, as I said we dated and had a good friendship. Any way, her brother had told me on numerous occasions that he was just waiting for his commission to come through, even though he was an attorney, I just kept my tongue in my cheek, and never expected to see him again when I left Shoemaker, that's the reason I couldn't believe what I was seeing.

He had been an attorney in San Francisco, and now he was assigned as the Port Director for the Admiralties, with responsibilities like assigning all shipping berths, and dock locations for all of the Allied shipping using this port. And of all things I was to be his Coxswain, putting the Harbor Pilots aboard every ship to enter this port. This was good duty and I enjoyed it for several months, before being transferred to a ship.

I went aboard the U.S.S. Stevens D. D. 479, a destroyer and one of the fastest ships in her class in the fleet, at that time. We were in a good many operations, from Guam to the Philippines, to Borneo, then back to the Philippines for some dry dock repairs. We were just ready to leave the dry dock the following morning, when we received word that the Japanese had surrendered and the war was over. As we left the dry dock the next morning we received orders to re-provision and go up into the China Sea to work with a group of mine sweepers in clearing and detonating mines in our assigned areas.

We had many interesting experiences while on this duty, not the least of which was when we ran into the midst of a mine field which didn't show on any of the available charts we had access to. We were successful in maneuvering out of the mines, and when we got a safe distance away we exploded them by firing into them. When we hit the first one they went off like a string of fire crackers, one right after the other until the entire field was gone. Needless to say we were all much more alert after that experience.

We stayed there for a short time then were sent to Tsing Tao, China to take over two Japanese ships and secure them so they could be returned to Tokyo. We secured them, turned them over to a British Cruiser, and we were immediately reassigned to Gin Sing Korea.

After about three weeks in Korea we received orders to return to the good old U.S.A., what a celebration we had that night, then we had to prepare for our return home. We returned to San Diego, by way of Guam, and Hawaii, with stops at each place for a few days. We also brought home a small group of Marines who were to be discharged when they returned.

When we returned back to the States we all got leaves so that we could be home for the holidays of either Christmas, or Thanksgiving, and then returned to the ship for routine duty once again. In March it finally came time for me to be discharged so I applied for my discharge in California, and it was approved, so I stayed there with my sister and her husband for a short while.

THE SCHOOL YEARS

I finally left California and headed back to Michigan, and on to college, I had fully intended to go to Michigan State College (now Michigan State University), but due to some political snags I couldn't get into a land grant college or university in Michigan without at least three years in a formal institution, and that was regardless of the fact that I had completed my high school, and had some college credits from U.S.A.F.I. (U.S. Armed Forces Institute), I could not qualify.

After exhausting every possible avenue I decided to go back to the basics and started high school over again. It was decided by the Superintendent and Principal that with my background I could take all of my classes in two years so that I would still have some credits from my G.I. Bill of Rights on education and could still get some college in after I finished high school.

Things were not to be that simple however, shortly after starting high school I met two people who would be a part of my life for many years to come. One of them was a man six years younger than I was but we struck up a friendship that very few people are able to enjoy. I was best man at his wedding, and he and his family were just as much a part of our family as we were a part of his. He was an only child and in some respects very spoiled, yet in most things he was very normal, and not at all spoiled. This friendship lasted for nearly fifty years until his death from a combined stroke, and a giant aneurysm in his abdomen, needless to say this was another difficult time for all of us, especially since his father had died in October of the preceding year.

The second of the people I met in school was my wife of fifty four years. Our first date was to what is called a Sadie Hawkins day affair, where the girl asks the man for a date, it was

15

a senior class roller skating party, since Louanna was a senior and I was not she asked me to attend with her and I accepted. It didn't take long and we decided that our lives were meant to be spent together and after this many years I believe we each made the right decision. The following spring while the senior class was away on a trip to Washington D. C. we eloped. Just imagine their surprise when her class mates returned and found her with another type of mate.

Since I was working for the summer on a construction job it meant a very short honeymoon of one week at a cottage on a lake not far from home, then we moved into a mobile home in her parents yard for the balance of the summer. In the fall of that year I went back to school, drove school bus and did other odd jobs through the school year, and then in the spring I graduated. Unfortunately after graduation normal jobs were hard to find so I wound up working for the railroad as a cook for the Gandy Dancer gang, (these are called in to do extra work that the regular crews cannot handle). Since their work is seasonal that job only lasted for the summer, and jobs were no better to find than they had been in the spring, so I just kept looking, but to no avail.

THE ARMY EXPERIENCE

After much thinking and discussion it was decided I would go back into the Navy, so I went to the recruiting office only to be told they didn't need non-coms, if I was interested I could go in as a Seaman Second Class, the lowest enlisted rank after Apprentice Seaman. Not feeling good about it I went next door to the Army office, and felt better when they said they would give me a Sergeants rating, and allow me to pick my unit of assignment.

I chose the Fourth Infantry Division, which was stationed in Fort Ord, California, and arrived there in November. I was immediately selected to go to Aberdeen Proving Grounds, Maryland for training in the Ordnance School there as a Small Arms Weapons Mechanic. Another Sergeant and I tied for first place in our class and by doing so we were automatically transferred to the Ordnance School as Instructors.

I stayed there training both officers and enlisted men for about six months, all of the time requesting transfer to a line company somewhere, just away from the Ordnance School. I guess the Commanding Officer finally got tired of seeing my name come across his desk so often, anyway one day at lunch break I was called to his office and informed that a good friend of his was forming a new Heavy Automotive Maintenance Company, in Fort Bliss Texas, and I would be taking seven men with me and would leave on the following Thursday, to arrive in Fort Bliss on Sunday.

I had to rush around and get Louanna home to Michigan, and get back before our departure date. I made it with little time to spare. We arrived in Texas just as we were scheduled to and were immediately sent to our new Company Compound, because there was no place else for us to stay. When we arrived at the compound we found there was no one there except us, so we set up our bunks and made ready for the night. While we were finishing setting up an officer walked in and we came to attention. He put us at ease and introduced himself as the new Commanding Officer, Captain C. C. Head. He asked for anyone with typing experience and it turned out that I was the only one who qualified.

This lead me to a new assignment as Company Clerk, then later on to being the Company Personnel Clerk, with responsibilities for the personnel records of all of the enlisted and officer personnel, it also lead to a promotion for me which made me happy as it was more money and Louanna could join me in Texas where we spent some very happy times together.

While there she became pregnant and this lead to another amusing situation, in her third month I woke up one morning sicker than the proverbial dog, but since I had drank a few drinks the night before I didn't think too much of it until it continued for several days, and then into a week. When it continued for several more days unabated I went on sick call to see if there was anything the medics could figure out. When the Doctor came in and started questioning me, he was a Lieutenant Colonel, and very well spoken of. Imagine my surprise when he suddenly burst out laughing uncontrollably, when he finally quieted down he asked me if my wife was pregnant, I said yes, and he told me he was her Doctor, and that I was having her morning sickness. What a relief, even if I didn't get over it for several weeks, but I finally did.

Later that year the Korean War broke out and our division was pulled out from the Post Ordnance position and deployed to overseas operations, as we were readying for boarding the troop train for Seattle, Washington to leave for Korea, Louanna decided it was time to deliver our premature daughter of only eight months. She was healthy if only five pounds, they did however put her in an incubator and gave her oxygen to keep her stable.

Regardless of this we left for Korea with Louanna's sister coming down to stay with her until she and the baby could travel back to Michigan. When we arrived in Ft. Lewis, Washington I was contacted by the American Red Cross and informed that my father was in a crises situation back home having been on the operating table for some twenty minutes without a heartbeat, and the doctors physically massaging his heart to keep it beating until it began to beat on it's own again. They recommended that I leave for home immediately.

When I applied for an emergency leave I was informed that the Adjutant Generals Office in Washington, D.C. had sent out a directive stating that no troops who were slated for overseas duty were to be granted a leave for any reason. This led to still another turn of events for me and my receiving a discharge and returning home, due to a quirk in a Special Regulation, which I qualified for, so I took advantage of it, obtained my discharge, and headed for home all in a matter of a few hours.

I was able to catch a Military Air Transport plane out to El Paso, Texas and immediately picked up Louanna, our new daughter, and Louanna's sister, and we piled into the car and headed for Michigan. The trip was quite uneventful, and we arrived in four days, nearly broke, but in good spirits. Our daughter Charlene traveled home in a large toilet tissue carton which was about three times larger than necessary, but it left lots of room for padding around her.

I had talked to my mother and sister several times and was assured we could take a few days for the travel and everything would be alright, so as soon as we arrived at Louanna's parents house we left Charlene with them and headed to the hospital to see Dad and the rest of the family. It was a good reunion and I

19

found Dad in good shape considering what he had been through, and he was well on the road to recovery.

HOME AGAIN

Now it was time to face the reality of civilian life again and start searching for a job and a place to live. My old friend from high school, Raymond found out we were home and came right over to tell me his dad had a job lined up for me where he worked if I was interested, I sure was and went to work at Motor Wheel Corporation immediately, and with a short training course was made an inspector on the night shift.

We found a small apartment, cheap, and moved in, buying used furniture to get us by, and started getting settled. My work went well and we were able to start saving some money, which as it turned out was a good thing, because after two months I was laid off, just the day before Thanksgiving, it was quite a blow but fortunately we had been able to save enough money to see us through for a time.

While working at Motor Wheel I had put in an application for employment at Oldsmobile Division of General Motors Corporation. I had a brother and my Dad worked there, and much to my surprise in January I received a call to come in for an interview. The result of that interview was that I was hired and started to work immediately as a non production sweeper, chip hauler. Not a very exciting job but it got me acquainted with the operations in the engine plant, and I found out that I was pretty good at straightening the rocker shafts for the engines, so while the regular operators were on break or at lunch, I would set at their presses and run production for them. As a consequence they were able to make their full production every day before quitting time.

When the boss found out what was happening he got me a replacement and put me on that job running production full time. This gave me a good pay raise, as well as a chance to show what

I could do. I established my seniority after ninety days and then shortly after that the steel industry went out on strike and I was laid off.

When I was called back it was in the government war production effort working on the 3.5 M.M. rockets. It was a good job but boring, until one day while I was running my press someone came up behind me and asked what in the world I was doing there and not in the Army. I turned around and there stood my old Company Commander from the day I arrived at Ft. Bliss. He was not a Captain any longer but was wearing two stars, and in command of the Ordnance Inspection teams for most of the states east of the Mississippi River, and was inspecting our facilities. Normally he would not go out into the plants but would go to the office section and look at the records, but for some reason that particular day he felt that he wanted to come out into the factory proper, and I'm sure glad he did.

While we talked I kept operating the press I was running and the Plant Manager, with his assistants, the Plant Superintendents, with their assistants, stood there watching and listening, wondering what was going on, then the General said, stop running that press and lets go sit down and get a cup of coffee and talk, when I told him that I couldn't the Plant Manager said yes you can, come on lets all go up to the cafeteria and have some coffee together. We all went and were served coffee and other goodies, and spent the rest of the day talking. When the General asked me about the operation as they pertained to the ordnance work I gave him a very factual report and when he wrote his findings they were as I had told him, and we received an excellent rating for our efforts. He also asked about Louanna, and our daughter and how they were doing. I told him both were doing good and that Charlene was growing too fast.

FROM PRODUCTION TO MACHINE REPAIR

Shortly after this I applied for and was accepted as an Employee in Training in the Machine Repair Trade. After several years as a Journeyman I was asked to take a written test to become a first line supervisor, I wrote the exam and shortly was sent into a six month training program before being put on as a supervisor.

In October of 1963 I went into a permanent salaried position and during the next nineteen years moved back across the main plant complex, which consists of some two dozen buildings situated on several acres of land. I was familiar with all of the Machine Repair Areas and so was utilized wherever a replacement was needed after my regular shift was ended. This led to much more experience and more responsibilities, which was fine with me since it also led to pay raises very frequently.

Shortly after I went on salary my immediate supervisor suggested that I write an entrance exam for a part time training program at General Motors Institute, in Flint, I did and was accepted into their Industrial Management Department. It only took me six years to complete the program and qualify for my Associates Degree, I felt pretty good about that since I was also working full time, after all it was only about twenty years later than I had planned, and in an entirely different avocation, but then it was college, and I did very well at it too.

MY CHANGED LIFE

Most of the time I spent on supervision was uneventful until on October 30, 1981, I came to know Jesus Christ as my Lord and savior, it was on a Sunday night, and I have not been the same since, and never can be again. I had been on a one week vacation a little over two weeks after my wife Louanna had accepted Him as Lord of her life, and I was sure in my own mind that if God was going to call me to His service it would be at a time when I could get used to my new life, before I went back into the plant to work. That just goes to show you how much my mind and Gods don't mesh.

When I was at the altar that night I had asked God to take away all of my desire for alcohol, and tobacco, from me, and He did, to this day I have never had the least desire for either one. The next morning I went into the plant extra early to get used to my new life as a Christian in that aspect of my life, there were some amusing experiences those first few day, but eventually my crew of skilled trades people accepted the idea of my changed life style and respected it as well.

HIS CALL

Where will you be when Jesus comes
Flying with Him or on the run
Seeking a place where you can hide
Since in His love you do not abide

When the Rapture comes will you go
To meet Him who loves you so
Go with Him to your home on high
Or will you most surely die

24

Won't you come to Him my friend
Receive His joy without an end
Let Him into your heart right now
Ask Him He will show you how

If not you have made a choice
You have not listened to His voice
Then surely you will burn in hell
All I can do then is wish you well

You did not heed His urgent call
Between you and Him it is a wall
Oh I beg you now my friend
Come before your life can end

About this time there was some talk that General Motors was going to offer an early retirement for salaried personnel so I started getting used to my new life by praying and asking God to have His was in this situation. If it was what He wanted then allow me to retire early, and to please open the door and allow it to happen, and to show me what it was He had for me to do, and if it was not His will for me to leave, then stop the possibility and show me what He wanted me to do inside the plant until it was time for me to move on.

On December twenty third of that year God not only opened the door, He slammed it back hard enough I thought the hinges might be broken. I had previously thought of retiring in August of 1982, but when God opened that door for early retirement it was with nearly four hundred dollars more a month to retire early, than I would have received if I had waited until August.

Needless to say I accepted the early retirement and my last official day at work was on February fourteenth, with my official retirement date as April first. As I bid farewell it was with mixed

25

emotions, since I had spent over thirty one years working there, and had met and worked with so many wonderful people.

After retiring I spent time working at our church doing routine maintenance work and just generally helping out where ever needed. From there I went on to other short time jobs around the area before I finally said that is enough, Louanna retired and we spent much of our time together, Charlene and her husband Bill moved in about a half mile from us and so we kept busy there helping them get settled in, then my friend Raymond came into the picture with his needs which kept me busy for ten years or so prior to his death. Since then I have devoted most of my time to pursuing God and His complete will in my life, through my devotions and prayer.

Since becoming a Christian I have tried to make my life so that every day is lived the same, given over completely to God. I try to make my life an act of devotion to God so that everything is done in His name, and for His glory. I don't mean by this that I haven't stumbled, or failed Him, what I am saying is that even when I fail He is a gracious and forgiving God who picks me up sets me back on my feet and forgives my transgressions, as I ask His forgiveness.

We should all realize that God alone is the reason for our very existence, for our prayers to acknowledge Him as the ruler of our lives, then to thank Him for His mercy and grace to us, with every breath we take. We should recognize that any way of life, any use of our time, our talents, or our money that is not in accordance to the will of God is a sure waste, not just of the one we fail to use in His will but all of them.

Our prayers should be in accordance to the will of God, so that we can live unto God in the same spirit that we pray unto Him. Is it because we lack this consistency that we see so much confusion in the lives of so many people? They are in Church on

Sunday morning, on time, singing hymns, and raising their hands in worship, then when they leave, it is "business as usual". Their life goes back to spending their time, money, life in general, in the cares, worries, and fears, their pleasures and indulgences, their labors, and diversions, exactly as the rest of the world. Actually they are a mockery before the rest of the world, mostly because the world is aware that the prayers of these people are like their devotions to God, sometimes, sometimes not.

THE SACRIFICE

The love I have for you oh Lord
Is not easy for others to know
To be holy and completely devoted
Working for the one who loves me so

You walk with me through the valleys
Or up on the mountains so high
You will never leave or forsake me
While I am alive or when I shall die

I serve you because I love you
I have no other earthly desire
Though you may let things beset me
And even try me by a great fire

For I'm saved by the grace of the Father
Who had you die on that cruel tree
To take the sins of the world upon you
And hang there for a wretch like me

What we need most of all is to be certain that our daily life, and our prayer life coincide with what God wants from us. Our daily walk with the Lord should be so close that whenever we meet some one, they would have to turn their face away, or ask us to cover ours, because the presence of God is so bright around

27

us, just as it was around Moses, and he had to cover his face when he came down from the mountain after spending time with God.

We need to be so different that we reject the things that the world calls good, we don't have to fear any of it's evils, we can reject it's joys and it's happiness, and become as new born babes, born into a new world, where we can live a life of Spiritual watching, Holy fear, and learning to live our life in a different world. To take up our cross daily, deny ourselves, forsake pride and vanity, to give up our whole lives to God and the furthering of His kingdom.

If self denial is to be a condition of our salvation, then doesn't it go without question that this same self denial must be a part of our every day life? If humility is a duty of every Christian then why not our every day life a life of humility? After all we have been told to dress the naked, nurture the sick, visit the prisoners, take in the homeless, are not these expressions of love, and shouldn't they be a constant part of our lives regardless of effort and self sacrifice?

Does God not want us to be contented, and thankful to Him in our every day lives, does He want us to be wise and holy, as the new born children of God? If this is true then we must renounce all that is vain, and foolish in every aspect of our daily lives. If we are indeed to be new creatures in Christ then our lives must show it to the world by living an exemplary life style every moment of every day. The point I am trying to make is that if Religion, or Christianity, hasn't changed a persons mind and attitude with respect to these things, what has it done for him?

Putting it another way, if a mans doctrines of Christianity were put into practice, and lived every day it would be as easy to know a Christian by the outward appearance as it is now difficult to find a person who lives the Christian life. Why is it that the lives of so many people who lay claim to the born again Christian experience, are so contrary to the very principles of their basic Christianity they claim?

Why is it a person can find it so easy to fall into the traps of Satan? Sins such as lying, stealing, unfaithfulness, homosexuality, cheating, drinking, drugs, and on into infinity, and at the same time find it so difficult to fully intend to serve God in a like manner? Even Clergymen are not immune to the wiles of the devil, there are as many who are given over to these same worldly enjoyments as there are people who are of the world. Even pornography on the internet is common among these so called Christians.

READY FOR BATTLE

Here I am right now my Lord
I stand here ready to obey
Whatever you would have me do
I only need to hear from you

I wasn't drafted into your army Lord
I reported for duty at your word
Please use me to help others see
The joy of serving one such as thee

The only one who can save from sin
If they will only let you come in
To fill their hearts with simple love
Sent by the Father from heaven above

Ready for battle at your command
Carrying your banner in lifted hand
Then when the time on earth is done
To know the battles have all been won

GODS EXPECTATIONS OF US

Is it a lack of dedication on the part of Christians, lack of teaching, understanding, or is it a lack of intention to even serve the God they claim to represent? The early Christians had every intention of not only serving God, but to sever family ties, and relationships, and doing everything in their power and ability to further the Church, even going so far as to die for that cause.

Are we sincere enough in our walk with the Lord to forsake all, take up our cross daily, and follow where ever God leads us, do whatever He tells us to do, and not look back longingly at the world, but be ready to die, if it comes down to that, for the cause of Gods calling? Are we ready to walk so closely with God that what ever He says is what we will do?

Are you willing to walk as if you had been brought up from infancy by Jesus Himself, and talk that way to every person you meet? Not only talk that way, but live that way, in every aspect of your life? In your business dealings, your visits, financial fortunes, personal energies, and time, since they are not your own, but belong to God anyway? Are you ready to look into the Scriptures to get every instruction relating to the proper use of your estate, deny yourself the personal pleasures, and indulgences you could have? Are you ready to present your all to God and say, how shall I use this to further your kingdom, and do your work oh Lord?

This is not something that just looks good in theory, but can't be put into practice because it has been done, not only in the past but is being done today by many people who have made it a point to please God in every one of their actions, both in public, as well as in their private lives.

Think seriously about a few things in our lives, are you and I contented to let the rat race of our everyday life rule us, are we satisfied that we spend our time, money, energies, and lives in a way that is pleasing to us, or do we spend them for God and the furthering of His kingdom? Do we seek to please God, and have the best and happiest life he has for us?

When we came to God through His Son, and received Him as our Lord and savior, didn't we have certain expectations of what God would do in our lives, and in us? I know I did, and as we study the word we come to realize that God has expectations from us, God expects our intentions to be what His intentions are for us.

God intends for us to live a Holy, and virtuous life every single day, He expects us to show forth His love, caring, understanding, and help for each other, regardless of whether or not others we know, fall short of these expectations. If we fall short God will remind us of these shortcomings, and show us what we should be doing about them, if we will only listen and act on His words of guidance.

DREAMS

Where will you take your dreams from here
Will you travel with them far or near
Can you sail among the clouds so high
Or will you let them fade and die

A dream is always so worthwhile
Sometimes it brings a tender smile
Other times it might bring a frown
This always drags your spirit down

31

So dream your dreams as they come
Entertain them all one by one
Then take the best and run with them
Show them you can become their friend

When it is time to lay them down
Do it with a smile not a frown
For this is how you are set free
To look for other dreams you see

If you haven't been able to become perfect yet, is that a reason to stop, or rather should you and I, not only strive to attain that perfection, but make it our full intention to diligently seek after it, and not neglect the seeking to eliminate any imperfections in our daily life? The scriptures point us to a life of continuous striving to maintain our salvation with all diligence, and with fear and trembling.

If my claim to Christianity is only a form, a membership in a Church, or an adherence to laws laid down by my Church, with no Biblical foundations, or rules and restraints, am I indeed a Christian, or am I just deceiving myself? Am I striving to enter in at the straight gate, or am I walking so closely to the line between it and the world as to be straddling that line, rather than fleeing away from it as far as I can get?

No matter how weak and imperfect we as humans might be, no matter how many times we may fail God, if we have done our utmost to please Him, we will be forgiven, and received by Him. If however we stop striving for human perfection then we have stopped short of what the scriptures require of us. How comfortable are you and I going to feel at the final hour of our life? Are we going to feel we have done everything it is humanly possible to do towards living a perfect Christian life, as the Holy Spirit directs us, or are we going to feel completely inadequate in our life long intention of pursuing Holiness? Can we honestly say we are living our lives as Gods word tells us to live them? Can we honestly say that every moment of every day we intend to live up to the gospel of Jesus Christ? Is our heart completely clear so that when the hour comes for us to pass on can we look forward to being with God in heaven, or must we look back over our shoulder, wishing we had earnestly attempted to live up to Gods expectations of us.

Have all of our dealings in life since we became Christians been honest, honorable, forthright, and charitable, or have we continued in the same old way, unscrupulous in our dealings in business, and other aspects of our daily life? You see laying on your death bed and reflecting on these things has to make us realize how petty our lives might have become if we put anything at all ahead of God and His words of life. Can I at this moment expect, and receive mercy from God?

HOW DO WE PLEASE GOD

How do we go about pleasing God so that we can expect His mercy to fall upon us? There is only one answer to that question, complete devotion and submission to Him. Everywhere we go, everything we see, every single aspect of our lives must be done unto God. Whatever it is must be as if it were a service to Him, in complete conformity to His will for each one of us.

We must all walk before God in the same Holy Spirit, forsaking our carnal self, our bad tempers, our fleshly lusts, and all of the sins of the world, which satan is continually bombarding us with, the turning completely, and devotedly into servants of God and of His holiness. If we seek after riches, fame, glory, or recognition, then we are not seeking or serving God, but other masters, and we cannot expect any title or reward from God in the after life.

GODS STRENGTH

God is my strength in time of trouble
He sends me help from heaven above
His light shines so I won't stumble
He always speaks of His great love

I will trust Him with my life
He will keep me from all sin and strife
I will seek Him every livelong day
He will always hear me as I pray

I will lift my voice in song
As He keeps me from all wrong
In times of battle He is my guard
He keeps me by His ageless word

I will always call on Him
He is my rock when things look dim
His hand is always out to me
Just try His great love and be set free

Regardless of what our employment is, if it is lawful it is our duty to God to live above the world, and not be of the world, no matter what. We must be directed totally and completely in preparing ourselves, and others for another better life. If our aim in this life is only to become wealthy, and indulge ourselves in the luxuries of the world, retire and spend our life on ourselves, not because God has blessed, but because we did it ourselves, we therefore earned the right to go our own merry way, we are not only mistaken, we are on our way to eternal damnation, unless we change quickly and completely. If we intend to live our lives for Christ we must, every moment of every day, in our employment, in our worship, both public and private, in short whatever we do, be certain it is devoted entirely to the glory of God.

God wants to be pleased with us whenever He looks at us, He wants to see us giving Him glory in everything we do and say. He wants us to be sure of our devotion and love in everything we say, do and even what our thoughts are, in a very realistic way God wants you, and I to do, say and think, as if He were visibly standing at our elbow every waking moment of our life. When we live our lives in this manner we can be sure he will be pleased.

Whatever it is that God has given us was, and is intended to be shared with those less fortunate than we are, whether it be our knowledge, wisdom, employment, residence or finances, we are intended not only to multiply them, but and of much more importance, to share them with others.

Whether we be laborers, or professionals, self employed, or working for another, we are to set the example of Christianity in all of our endeavors. Doctors, Attorneys, Engineers, Bankers, Carpenters, Mechanics, Bookkeepers, or any other employment, carries the same responsibility as did the three servants who received the talents, not just to keep our resources as the one did, but, to multiply them for Gods kingdom.

The talent spoken of in this parable is of the monetary variety, but God gave those talents we have, to be nurtured and shared, passed on to the next generation, so that they too might have the opportunity to share with the succeeding generation. There is one stipulation in all of this, which must not be forgotten, it is, always thank God for what He has given, and for the opportunity to pass it on to some deserving, less fortunate person. Give God the glory for all of His gifts, and talents, which you have gained from His service.

Since we are all created by God, and in His image, we are therefore intended to be servants of God. Using the talents God has provided us with to do for others who can't do for them selves, or can't hire some one to do for them, is another way God uses His people, and blesses them for using their talents as He has shown us. Psalm 1:6, says it best, "For the Lord knoweth the way of the righteous, but the way of the ungodly shall perish". Be sure to strengthen you life and therefore your soul, with good works, prayer, peace and wisdom, by reading and meditation, and feed it to the fullest by learning and practicing Gods love, keeping your soul in His presence, and beholding His face.

HIS PEACE

Let not your heart be troubled
Cast all of your cares on me
I will make all of your burdens lighter
Trust me and you will see

I took all of those stripes upon me
All of your sins became mine you see
Now you can walk on freely
Because of what I did for thee

Oh come to me all ye sinners
Ask my forgiveness at the Cross
The time is passing by so swiftly
Your soul need not be tempest tossed

I will give you the peace you are after
Take all of your burdens for my own
Come to me ask for my forgiveness
As you kneel before my throne

LIVING IN HIS PRESENCE

Is there really any reason why we don't need to act as if we were in Gods presence at all times? After all His presence is everywhere, and He has given us what ever we possess, so we need to live unto Him wherever we are, and whatever we are doing. Everything about us should reflect God in us at all times, in all situations, we must look up to Him and measure our own precepts of the gospel against the things Christ taught and lived when He walked on the earth. What will I wish for more of when I am ready to depart this world, will it be more of the things of this world, or more of the wisdom and holiness of God?

Since everything we have was given us by God, it is only reasonable for us to assume not only that we are servants of God, but that all we possess as a gift from Him shall be returned to God and His use to advance the kingdom. The blessings that will flow from this use of Gods gifts to us are beyond our ability to understand, and these same blessings will continue to multiply as we continue to follow Gods ways, and doing it all in a genuine reflection of Gods divine love in us to all others. God tells in Matt. 6:19-21, not to lay up treasures here on earth, so just let Gods gifts to us flow through us with His love in our hearts, flowing through us to others. In Proverbs 19:17, we read, "He that hath pity upon the poor lendeth unto the Lord; and that which he hath given will He pay him again: Just think of the opportunity this gives us for lending to the Lord. The poor are always with us, and around us, so we have a glorious means to not only help someone in need, but also to lend to God with the full expectation that He will repay us everything given in His name and in His love.

Using the money God has entrusted to us on our own personal desires and wishes, will have the effect of corrupting us and leading us away from God and into the ways of the world, and the things we are to be speaking out against. Spending our money only on ourselves is only going to hurt us, and harden our hearts to the point where we would not want to help others, and still expect to have God bless us.

Matt. 25:31-46, tells us of the "Son of Man", coming to sit on the throne of His Glory, and separating us as a shepherd separates his sheep from the goats, the sheep on His right hand, and the goats on His left. Then the King will call to those on His right hand to inherit the kingdom prepared for them (us), because we fed Him, clothed Him, visited Him when He was sick, and went to prison to visit Him. When they asked how they had done all of these things He told them since they had done it to the least of His brethren they had done it unto Him. But those on His left hand had done none of these so He told them to depart from Him into everlasting punishment, while those on the right hand were sent into eternal life and joy with their Lord.

I don't know how God could have made His instructions to us any clearer than those scriptures do. It doesn't say it is a recommendation, or a suggestion, and it isn't just to be an occasional piece of charitable work it is meant to be a continual, day by day exercise in every day of our lives, to the fullest extent of our ability to perform it. When we love God with all of our heart, our mind, and our strength, it seems only natural to assume we will do these things every day of our existence, just as an example to the world, of what Gods love truly is, if for no other reason.

Other than prayer and devotion I think two things which every Christian must adhere to are a strict use of our time and our money, these two talents are a constant source of blessings, not only to ourselves, but to others when they are properly used, and can rapidly propel us along the way to becoming more Christ like every day that we pursue them. If we ask ourselves how to make the most of our short lives, and to be happy in our every pursuit, we need only remember God requires us to be completely devoted to Him and His commands, following His will in our lives.

FOLLOWING AFTER JESUS

If we will renounce the world, and follow Christ, we will find ourselves moving closer to Him, and as we do we will come to realize that our entire being belongs to God, and what ever we do, think, or say, needs to be as unto Him. When we look at someone and get upset because he or she spends their money on drugs, or drinking, or gambling, rather than to care for themselves, or their family, what do we look like in Gods eyes, if we use what He has given us, to indulge in our own lusts, of clothes, or cars, or homes, rather than for His use and glory?

Can we, each individual say, as they read this, that they have renounced the world to follow Jesus in the exercise of humility, charity, devotion, abstinence, and heavenly pursuits, or are we only partially sold out to Him, and are holding back in some areas of our life? Do we consider ourselves a complete servant of God here on this earth, to be His hands, feet, eyes, and ears to help others?

Do we arise in the morning full of the joy of the Lord with prayers for the day, and great expectations for God to reveal to us His plans for the day in our lives, waiting to see who we will meet that needs something we can offer them? Do we see lost souls on the street who need the savior, or is there someone who needs some type of monetary relief? Do we go forth to work with such joy our fellow workers cannot help but know we are different, and not only envy us our joy, but want to have it for themselves? And are we ready, and willing to tell them what it is that gives us our joy?

Are we going to live our lives according to the word of God, or are we going to live them according to the world? If we are going to live according to Gods word we have a complete guide for our everyday life, every moment of every day. We must

41

abstain from idols, fornication, all appearance of evil, and fleshly lusts. As we ask we shall receive, so ask for life for backsliders, and loved ones, all of these things and hundreds more are spelled out in the New Testament as commands from God.

THANKSGIVING

A day we have for giving thanks
To the Lord for all that He has done
The things that He has given us
The victories in battles He has won

He showers on us His perfect love
Gives us sweet glimpses of heaven above
He guides the pathway we will trod
Through His spirit by our loving God

So we give thanks to you oh Lord
You are ever true to your holy·word
It is our guiding light each new day
We lift our hearts to you and pray

So give ye thanks to the Lord
All creatures here on this earth
For God came here and died for you
That your life would have great worth

Are we glad for everything God has done in our lives, our world, work hobbies, family, and so forth? Do we give Him praise for all of this, or do we just take it for granted, that it is by some right? If God created us and loves us, why wouldn't He be totally interested in every aspect of our life? We know He does because He has told us to be perfect even as our Father in heaven is perfect.

Do we have a fault against some one, or does someone have a problem with us? If so when we bring an offering to the Altar of God if we are reminded of it we are to leave the offering there, go and find the brother or sister in Christ, and reconcile our difference, then, and only then do we return to the altar and present our sacrifice to God.

Do we do everything to the glory of God, whether it be at a meal, talking with a friend or acquaintance having a cup of coffee, or just as we start our day? Is everything we do tested against Gods word, so that when we read, we feel we are sitting at the feet of Jesus as He instructs us, His Disciples?

When we see someone who is off from work, with no insurance, or income, are we quick to come to their aid, so that the family doesn't need for medicine? Or do we pass by on the other side, and let the proper agencies take care of that brothers and his family, if there are any available to help them? In the parable of the good Samaritan, Jesus describes how some so called Christians react to such situations, the Priest and the Levite passed by on the other side of the road and left the man to die, while the Samaritan not only went out of his way to help, he even paid the lodging at the inn, and agreed to pay more if due. Where do we fit into this situation, are we Priest, Levite, or Samaritan?

When Christ says in Luke 9:23, "If any man will come after me, let him deny himself, and take up his cross daily, and follow after me" do we do this? Or do we follow Him as long as it feels good, or suits our needs, or is convenient for us, and then when we feel that is not the way for us, do we forsake Him, go our own way, and do as we want? If when we start out to follow Jesus we don't intend to follow Him all the way, why do we pick up that cross to begin with?

Self denial is a part and parcel of our every day life as Christians, it started in the Old Testament with Abraham, Moses, Samuel, Esther, Ruth, and so many others, who set the example for us, then it carried on into the New Testament with the Apostles, and even included the denial of life itself where most of the Apostles were concerned. When we pick up our cross today are we prepared to follow Jesus all the way regardless of cost, can we deny ourselves to the point of death for the cause of taking Jesus to the world? It is quite possible this could happen in this world today, things are changing so rapidly here in this country we may soon be denied our right to worship as we wish, or where or when we wish. Can we be strong as Daniel was, and trust in God to deliver us from these things, or will we be weak, and succumb to the pressures of the world?

You say how can we live in today's society as the Apostles did, things are so much different now than they were then, we can't live the life they lived? Their lives and behavior is the common example that all Christians should have. It is their spirit, and love of God we are to imitate, not necessarily their life style. If we will act as they did, with complete submission to the direction of God and the leading of the Holy Spirit, then we can look forward to mighty works being completed in our life for the glory of God. Sacrificial giving, self denial, renunciation of the world, and spreading the love of God to the lost, is really what is expected of us if we are going to call ourselves Christians, and be suitably prepared for the life eternal with our Lord and Savior.

If we are going to live our lives Holy, and acceptable unto God then our use of every part of our resources must be a complete devotion of every part and parcel of them to God, if men are to be exacting and honest in their every day living, then how much more are we as Christians, to live our lives above, and beyond even the slightest amount of criticism by anyone?

As we start our day do we go about looking for ways to serve God, help others, and in general make the world a better place for all, or do we look away from someone in obvious need, go our own way, and leave the world the same or in even worse shape than it was when we awoke? Jesus told us to go and do unto others as we would have them do unto us. Do we want to have someone look away when we need assistance, or would we rather that they would come near, and give us the help we need? Can we find it in ourselves to speak a kind word to a hurting soul? Can we take that elderly person shopping? Can we reach out to that troubled youth, and give something besides despair? All of these things, and oh so many more fall within our Christian walk, and should be a vital part of our daily life? Don't ask or even think, what's in it for me, simply ask what will this action on my part do for them and the furtherance of Gods kingdom?

Can we possibly as Gods children let His love flow through us, transcending all race, color, class, and culture? Our very salvation requires our loving one another as God loves us. If we are unable to love our neighbor, the person across town, the ghetto resident, the wealthy, or middle class, the homeless, then how can we ever fit together, or be one body, and worship God the creator in His heaven? Is it possible for us to bring about a world where this is the norm? Is it possible to start over with a new generation, teach them love, respect, honor and hope, according to Gods principals, that they might lead each succeeding generation into the same peaceful, loving path?

My heartfelt prayer is that we as Christians will do these things as Gods word commands us to do and lets see if we can make this world the way it once was when God walked with Adam and Eve here on this earth and communed with them in the cool of the evening. As we go forth remember that it is through His love for us that we have the air we breathe, the home we live in, and the food on our tables, as well as the clothing on our bodies. Let us use everything that He has given us to bless and be a blessing to all of those we meet along the way in our daily walk with Him.

THE GARDEN

When God breathes life into a soul
He opens a door to make him whole
There is a garden behind that door
With flower seeds planted upon the floor

As the soul grows and cultivates them
Their beauty springs forth to glorify Him
Not in straight rows but scattered all about
Each blossom a beauty with never a doubt

As we go through our garden of life
We can pick a bouquet to give a friend
Then this beautiful garden will never end
It will live on again and again

First pick the flower of kindness
To give to some poor hurting soul
Let kindness to others be normal
In service to help them to be whole

Then add to the bouquet great loving
Present it with those already given
For this is the greatest of all gifts
Coming straight from our Father in heaven

Then when this life is over
And God tightly closes our door
We can see the garden that is planted
As we walk along that heavenly shore

SERVICE UNTO GOD

Charles (Chuck) A. De Land

HIS ARMS

Reclining in the arms of my Jesus
Always gives my soul it's perfect rest
I am refreshed and go forth blessed
Into the battle of each new day

I take God's word into the land
Just the way my Lord has planned
As I go He is my faithful guide
Then in His love I will abide

As the dark speaks to the dark
And the morning star to the light
The only one who stands for right
He alone takes all my fears away

So I'll go forth in His abiding love
Knowing it comes from heaven above
Take His love where ere I go
That from my heart His love will show

49

SERVICE UNTO GOD

Are we ready to obey God as Moses and Joshua did, are we going to serve Him and go forth as He tells us, when He tells us? If we will only learn to follow every step of the divine direction of God we will have the same successful outcome of our every endeavor for Him. There are many instances where success came by obeying God's every command. There are also many more instances where failure was the result of disobedience.

There are also instances of failures where the people went off on their own when God did not give them directions. Every one of there examples are recorded for our profit, if we will listen and heed God's leading and guidance, as children of God it is imperative that we be led by God, and His Spirit, living and walking in the Spirit, meditating in His word and obeying it at all times if we expect to be successful followers of God.

God loves obedience much more than worship because obedience means we are sold out to Him regardless of cost, or appearance in the human state, and how it may appear to man. This is to be a constant thing, not just Sunday, but every day of our lives, every moment of our waking hours. Josh. 1:8, states Gods word to His people through His leader Joshua, "This book of the law shall not depart out of thy mouth; but thou shalt meditate therein day and night, that thou mayest observe to do according to all that is written therein: for then thou shalt make thy way prosperous, and then thou shalt have good success". This is the secret of obedience and this in turn will bring you success in your every endeavor.

Righteousness comes from obedience and must be cultivated and nurtured by Gods word at all times, and will in turn bring about a rich, fruitful, Christian life. On the other hand, Psalm 1:4, tells us that, "The ungodly are not so: but are like the chaff which the wind driveth away". These wicked or unrighteous are as the grass that soon withers, or as wild beasts who disregard all decency and do their own thing regardless of the consequences, filled with the vanity of their own minds and knowledge rather than that wisdom which comes from God.

If we will follow after Gods word, and way, we will have no condemnation, however if we walk in our own way after the lusts of the flesh we will be condemned to death, and eternal fire. God's way gives us the strength to overcome the sins of the world, and complete deliverance from them, as we go about our daily life in His way. Christ was able to walk on this earth, in real live flesh, and walk without the sins of this world, and He made us a way where we do not have to continue in our sins.

Jesus did this because He didn't submit to satan and his sinful nature. Jesus came to earth through a woman, but He was not the seed of a sinful man, but of God, who did not curse the children of women, but of God's first creation of humans, man, He then passed this on to his children. Mary was only a means for God to bring His son into this world as a human body, to live without sin, He was conceived by the Holy Ghost, not by a sinful man.

OUR KING

The night of your birth
Dear lamb from above
The angels all gathered
To sing of your love

The Messiah had come
That the profits did say
Would be born in a stable
Laid in a manger of hay

51

To walk on this land
Where all men had trod
To bring man His salvation
This dear Son of God

The shepherds all gathered
As the angels did say
In a Bethlehem stable
You will see where He lay

Fear not go and worship
Bow down at His bed
Your new King is worthy
As the prophets have said

So worship Him freely
All men here on earth
To prove yourselves worthy
Of Emmanuel's birth

WALK IN THE SPIRIT

In Gal. 5 we find that if we will only walk in the Spirit, we will not fulfill the lusts of the flesh, because the flesh is completely contrary to the Spirit, this does not mean that we are without hope because Gods Grace, and our continual seeking for perfection is our hope and eternal victory.

Even though the works of the flesh bring temporary pleasure we must flee from them, such things as adultery, fornication, uncleanness, lasciviousness, witchcraft, envying, murder, drunkenness, and many others, if we do these things we will not inherit the kingdom of God. On the other hand, the fruit of the Spirit is, love, joy, peace, longsuffering, gentleness, goodness, and faith in God and His love and concern for our well being at all times.

We must crucify our flesh daily, every time a sinful thought comes into our mind we must crucify it, and above all do not act upon it. If we give in to these things, even the smallest of them, which seem to be insignificant, we will soon begin to harden our hearts and not stay true to our salvation, which was purchased by Jesus on the Cross. It is a constant battle to stay pure and holy before God, but the victory will bring great rewards. God will always give us a way of escape from every temptation we face if we will only call on Him in Jesus name.

In Jere.17:9, we read that, " The heart is deceitful above all things, and desperately wicked: who can know it"? If our natural heart is this wicked how can we without Gods help keep it under complete subjection to His will? If we don't take the time to discipline our hearts, and minds they will become wild and go any place they want to go and lead us to complete destruction, we must train ourselves to take time every day to read the Bible, pray for Gods guidance, and meditate in His word and love.

Charles (Chuck) A. De Land

OUR SINS ARE FORGIVEN

When Jesus died on the Cross, for you and I, He not only cleansed us from our sins, He also gave us the staying power we need to maintain that salvation every day. Each of us has a will, and that will is so overcome by the lusts of the sins of this world that alone we are helpless. If our will, and heart will remain on God and we will consent to His will and law then the evil slave master, Satan cannot deceive us into his ways of lust and sin. It is imperative that we not only love God, and serve Him, we must also delight ourselves in Him, and our service to Him. There is victory over sin, and through Christ we can attain that victory.

As Christians we are not overcome by the things of the flesh for we are of the Spirit, if the Spirit dwells in us, if Christ is truly in us then our body is dead to all sin, and the Spirit will dominate our lives, and our lives will then be pure, and it will be dead to all sin, and our lives will be the righteous life God desires for us. With Christ in us the flesh has no more control over us for we have put our fleshly practices to death and walk in the light and love of God.

BACK AGAIN

So you turned away from Him again
The one who saved you from your sin
How does it feel to break his Heart
That loving friend who will not depart

Don't you know He cries for you
His gentle heart keeps on loving you
He will never turn away you see
His love for you is always free

So turn your heart back to Him
Before the vision He gave grows dim
Come fall upon your knees today
Ask His forgiveness as you pray

Then praise His name for His love
Sent from the Father in heaven above
For any time that you may stray
His forgiveness is but a prayer away

If Christ went to the cross and died for us while we were still living in sin, ungodly and therefore enemies of God, how much more will He do for us after we come to Him, repent of our sins, ask forgiveness and complete reconciliation with God? By serving us through His death, how much more is He able to serve us by His life living in us? When we receive the abundance of Gods grace, and His righteousness we will then reign victorious through Jesus Christ.

When we stop and consider the many reasons for not living in sin, and the benefits of living in a righteous way we must admit they are many. Death to sin nullifies death in the spirit, so we have resurrection from spiritual death, we walk in the newness of life, able to walk as Jesus did on earth, we have crucified our flesh from sin and it has no more dominion over us. We become married to Jesus and are free from the law of sin, and we are spiritually minded.

Gods mighty power raised Jesus from the grave, and this same power will raise the souls of sinners to make them new creatures in Christ as they come to Him for forgiveness. Just as Jesus died for the sins of this world once and for all so we are able to die unto sin once and for all and live for God forever. Sin is a tyrant that has the souls of man captive just as a slave is a captive to the one who owns him, body and soul, completely dominating in whatever life it touches. God delivers us from sin when we are born again, and if we enter back into sin it is our own choice and we have turned our back on God.

OBEDIENCE

We are not under the law that demands obedience without giving us the power to obey, we are under grace that demands obedience to God, given free pardon for our sins and the power to obey God and not Satan We cannot be a servant of Satan and sin, and a servant of righteousness, and Jesus at the same time. If we do commit sin we are a servant to that sin and Satan and not of Christ and the Righteousness of God.

We have been called by the Holy Spirit, set apart, put into a die and stamped with the image of God and Jesus Christ, therefore we are now stamped in their image, and as we grow and mature, the word of God is stamped on our hearts for eternity. Just as before we yielded our bodies to sin we must now yield them completely to holiness and righteousness, led by the Holy Spirit unto the truths of God.

God has chosen every person to salvation, and service to Him, He has also given every one a completely free will, and they can either accept or reject His call. Those who accept His call are conformed to the image of His Son, accepting Him as Lord of their lives, asking for forgiveness, and being cleansed of their sins by the blood of Jesus. Those who live and walk in the Spirit will not be separated from Christ, as long as they continue to walk in the Spirit. His Father, God is a sovereign God and He has ordained that salvation is only possible through His Son Jesus, and only then by conforming to His laws.

MY MANSION

I am looking for that mansion
Built on that street of purest gold
And when I cross that crystal river
All of heavens beauty will then unfold

That mansion He has built for me
While I am here upon this earth
Because His love is mine you see
And gives my life such matchless worth

Until I glimpse that home dear Lord
Please show me what I am to do
As I walk upon this sinful earth
My hearts desire is serving you

Then when my journey here shall end
I'll see your lovely face my friend
And throw myself into your embrace
To know that I have won the race

Eternal life is a gift from God free for us by His Grace, we as humans warrant hell, not eternal life with Christ, but He has purchased life eternal for us on the Cross. By the same token sin will take full advantage of the helpless state of man and deceive and kill us as we serve it. Sin can overpower our will and our reasoning and turn us away from God if we do not keep His word stamped on our hearts.

We Christians must not under any circumstances be minding the things of the flesh, but of the Spirit, if the Spirit dwells in us. If Christ is in us our bodies are dead to all sin and Gods Spirit dominates our lives as we live in righteousness. So if we are filled with the Spirit we don't owe the flesh a thing, and we are free to live a life completely free from sin.

Jesus the Messiah was sent to earth not as a Prince and mighty conquering warrior, that people would follow after Him for this very reason, yet the ones who followed Him then, and have since that time, cannot be counted by human means, but

God knows every one who has followed Him and will in the future.

GOD IS MERCIFUL

God will not ever harden against a person unless that person hardens their heart against Him, if they will seek His mercy God will show them great mercy. God is always righteous in His judgment and if men will humble themselves and call to Him and seek His mercy, He will show them great mercy. This leaves the responsibility of Gods mercy up to the individual. They can either humble their hearts, and receive His mercy, or they can exalt themselves and receive His judgment. God gave us free wills to either choose to serve Him, or refuse His mercy and serve His enemy, the devil.

God also uses the words stiff necked about those who refuse to hear His word and repent of their sins, they prefer going their own way and living in their sins rather than give up their stiff necked way, and letting God put His yoke on their necks, for His yoke is easy, and His burden is light. For your own sakes I pray that you will soften your stiff neck, and go after God with all of your heart, mind, and soul.

When you think of the Grace God has given to man by sending His Son to die for our sins, on a cross that was meant only for the vilest criminals, and yet Jesus was a sinless sacrificial Lamb for the sins of every man, woman, and child, from the time He was Crucified until He comes again it is a very sobering thought. When it comes time for you to die that is what you will be throughout eternity, when you take your last breath here on earth you cross over from mortality into immorality, and then it is too late to repent of your sins, and serve Jesus here on earth.

FAITH

We live by faith by faith alone
Till God calls us to our heavenly home
He gave to us the earth to rule
With His wisdom He gave His winning tools
A book that tell us how we must live
A suite of armor did He give
The dark world cannot enter in
Our faith will keep us from it's sin

We live by faith by faith alone
His guiding light will see us home
Help us build a wall oh Lord
For the building blocks we'll use your word
Help us to build it high and wide
That we may come to you inside
Then when we have learned to stand alone
Your word will guide us to our new home

In Prov. 12:1, God tells us, "Whoso loveth instruction loveth knowledge: but he that hateth reproof is brutish". The word brutish in this instance means he is as stupid as a wild beast. What God is trying to point out to us is that if we won't listen to His word, and His voice, even if it is from a human, and we will not repent but harden our hearts when we receive that admonition from Him we are like a wild, stubborn, nontrainable beast.

As long as we abide in God and His goodness and grace, we will be grafted into the vine, and kept secure in Gods love. We are meant to be a Holy Sacrificial Lamb to God, laid on the Altar just as the sacrifices of the early Israelites were brought to the Altar, we are now wholly the Lords for all time, and to conduct ourselves in a manner that will bring glory to God in our every word, action, and deed.

We must present our bodies a living sacrifice, holy, and acceptable to God, being His servants, subject to His direction at all times, not conforming to the ways of the world, for through salvation we are transformed from the world. As we fix our eyes on God, and follow His guiding light we can be assured that He will protect and keep us, not only here on this earth, but throughout eternity. You see God is always speaking to us, exhorting us and comforting us as we follow Him.

God cares for us in every way, and as long as we follow Him He will take care of our every need, no matter what it might be. His love is so all encompassing that He only sees the best that is in our hearts. As we visit our sick and hurting brothers and sisters in Christ, He goes with us and gives us the words and sympathetic heart we need to cheer them.

LIVE IN FAITH

Having moved ourselves out of Gods way and living in complete faith that He will carry us through every situation, and meet our every need we can just go forward in His love, serving Him, and worshiping Him in every thing we do and say. Go into the world and be the hands and feet of Jesus in this world, showing His care and concern in very real ways.

In closing I must ask some questions, not only of the reader but also of myself. What do you see as you look out the window of your home? In the springtime do you see the beauty of the renewing of the earth and the promise of His continual renewing of our lives every day? Spring with the promise of new growth budding forth in the plants and trees, flowers, and lawns. Is it a time of hope in the renewing of our own lives not only in Christ but in our minds and hearts as we view Gods infinite love for us?

In summer do you see the trees and flowers arrayed in all of their glory, the leaves on the trees fully matured and singing their praises to the Lord as the gentle breeze flutters them as it goes past? The flowers in full bloom, showing forth the beauty and colors of Gods Glory, which He reveals in all things, including us if we will let Him?

In autumn God has chosen to show us the beauty of preparing to rest and regain our strength, the fields have ripened for the harvest and the harvesters have worked hard to gather in the fruits of their labors, and Gods goodness for increasing their seed, just as He has prepared souls for the harvest, which is to come. He has promised that He will pour out His Spirit upon all flesh as the time draws nearer for His return, which according to all indicators is very soon. Are we working in the harvest and helping Him to reap the souls He has prepared and spoken to us about?

63

In winter when the earth lays dormant God continues to nurture His creations to prepare them for spring once again. In some areas He merely has the plants, flowers, and trees stand still, in others He covers them with a blanket of snow, which replenishes the water supply as it melts off in the spring. You see everything God does is pointed at spring, just as Jesus went through these same seasons in His life. Have you ever considered this thought?

Have you seen and grasped His love and forgiveness that you might have a springtime renewing of your life, with His forgiveness of your every sin? I pray that this may be so today if not.

One further question and I am finished, "What does God see in you as He looks out of His window in heaven"? Is it one who is wholly devoted to Him, one who does His bidding as He speaks, prays continually for guidance in your every action? Or is it one who obeys sometimes, and when he is ready to obey? I pray that the latter is not the case for this is a path that will lead to disregard of Gods commands and into an ultimate spiral of sin which will pull you in as a whirlpool, and never let you escape.

JESUS IS COMING AGAIN

SOON!!!!

Charles (Chuck) A. De Land

THE HAMMER

How did it feel to wield the hammer
That nailed your savior to the cross
Live in such a sin filled manner
It cost the Father this great loss

We all have sinned says the Lord
Yet Christ our debt has paid
The hammer was each sin we sinned
Through Him Gods plan was laid

We come to God through Jesus blood
His wounded side flowed as a flood
He never cried out or closed His hand
Such was His love for mortal man

The hammer was taken away you see
The moment your sins were forgiven thee
Now you need not feel the pain
His forgiveness makes you whole again

JESUS IS COMING AGAIN

SOON

HIS SECOND COMING

If you are a believer that the Bible is the inherent word of God, and that everything in it either has come true or will come true in the future, what would you consider as one of the most important events yet to take place? Would it be space exploration, or some new computer process, or do you think it would really be the Second Coming of Jesus as He said?

It is a fact, Jesus is coming again, and in Rev. 22:12, He says "Behold I come quickly". Knowing this, it is of the utmost urgency that we recognize our complete dependence on Him and the Holy Spirit for Gods glorious truths to penetrate our hearts. We have to learn to lean on Him and depend on Him for our every need. He will open your heart and mind to the complete understanding you need.

Jesus opened the understanding of His Disciples that they might understand the scriptures, and in Acts, He also opened the eyes and heart of Lydia so that she might receive the truth. The Holy Spirit is our teacher, guide, and comforter, and He will teach us as we welcome Him in this ministry.

We must hide the word in our hearts, and let the Holy Spirit water and germinate His life giving power in our lives. We need so much more in our lives than the mere intellectual thoughts of the truths of His coming, we must know without a doubt in our hearts, and change our lives in such a radical way as to completely turn from all of our wicked ways and listen to the revelation of the Holy Spirit as He speaks to our hearts.

The plan of Satan is and always has been to divide God's Children over unimportant and nonessential things pertaining to spreading God's gospel, his aim is to get God's people to waste time, money, strength, and even lives, over things that don't mean a thing, and gives Satan and his demons opportunity to laugh fiendishly. So while we saints are squabbling over this nonsense they can have a jubilee.

I believe the main question each of us needs to ask ourselves is, am I ready for Jesus coming again? What a solemn question that is to put to ones self. Am I walking as God has directed His saints to walk, does the thought of His coming make me apprehensive in any aspect of my life, private, personal, home life, business dealings? Am I meeting my responsibility to my family, my Lord, my neighbors, to all of the lost souls around me, and scattered abroad over all the earth, am I really ready?

How exciting to think of all the beauty and glory surrounding the coming of Jesus, yet we must not live in the same old unconcerned manner we have become accustomed to. We must have a deep burden for lost souls. We must reach out to not only the lost but also to those who have known the Lord and then for some reason have backslidden into a life of sin. We must fast and pray for a revival, not only in the land but in our own hearts, we must deny ourselves, all of the luxuries we hold dear and send the Gospel to the lost nations of the world.

CONFESSING TONGUES

Soon every tongue will confess
God says every knee shall bow
Then every Christian on earth will know
They have stayed true to Him somehow

When that great day arrives at last
We will join that happy throng
Every heart will be filled with joy
Our voices will burst out in song

When Jesus says this is the time
Come up and share my love divine
That is the time when every tongue
Will confess He is the promised one

So come to Him do not dismay
For He alone can take your sins away
Then you can be among that happy throng
Praising Him in heaven all eternity long

The soon coming of Jesus is a very serious thing for every Christian and must be considered intensely and thoroughly, it must explode in our hearts to the point it will radically alter our entire being as a Christian. We can't be satisfied over the coming of Jesus as a little child playing their favorite game as long as there are still lost souls around us. Let the Holy Spirit convict our hearts to the point where we will never be the same again, unable to settle down to the happy go lucky, easy going life we have in the past, but that our lives will be given in loving service to the one who loved us enough to die a cruel death on a cross for each of us.

Three different times in the twenty second chapter of the Revelation, Jesus declared, " I come quickly", He will come to earth again in person. When He came to walk on earth the first time He came as the Sacrificial Lamb, our redeemer, the next time He will come to reign as King of Kings, and Lord of Lords. No crown of thorns for His head, no nails to pierce His hands and feet, but as King of the earth, to reign eternally.

GOD'S WITNESS OF HIS WORD

In John 14:1-3 Jesus has encouraged each of us with simple words, telling us not to let our hearts be troubled, we believe in God, se should believe also in Him, and that He is going to prepare a place for us in His Fathers House, and if He goes to prepare a place for us He will come again and receive us that we might be with Him. What a testimony this is to His saints who await His coming.

If we were in a court of law in this country, and were calling on witnesses to back up our claim that Jesus is going to return to earth in all His Glory we could call on any number of witnesses, but lets start off with James and ask what he might say; "Be patient therefore brethren, unto the coming of the Lord, be also patient; establish your hearts for the coming of the Lord draweth nigh".

Now lets see what Job might have to say on this same witness stand: after all of his problems he could still state emphatically even though he was looking forward through the years, "For I know that my redeemer liveth, and that He shall stand at the latter day upon the earth; And though after my skin worms destroy this body, yet in my flesh shall I see God; whom I shall see for myself, and mine eyes shall behold, and not another's". Seeing all of this through the spirit, and giving this testimony even though Satan had buffeted him, taken his family, possessions, and caused devastating illness to come upon him Job could still through his faith make these positive statements.

Now how about calling Paul and see what he might say about the Lords returning. "For the Lord Himself shall descend from heaven: and the dead in Christ shall rise first; then we which are alive and remain shall be caught up together with them, so shall we ever be with the Lord. Wherefore comfort one another with these words". Can we possibly follow these words Paul has spoken and comfort those who are less fortunate than we are?

THE VALLEY

As we walk through that final valley
So full of fear and so all alone
If we will walk our walk with Jesus
He will see us safely home

Throughout our lives He is with us
Always carries our burdens and cares
If we will only trust Him
All of our cares and needs He shares

So walk through that final valley
With the Savior close by your side
There is never need to fear then
For in His arms you can ever hide

We might also call on some of Gods angels to take the witness stand and testify to the fact they stood on a hill and watched Jesus as He went up into heaven and asked the disciples standing there gazing up after Him, "Ye men of Galilee, why stand ye gazing up into heaven? This same Jesus which is taken up from you into heaven, shall so come in like manner as you have seen Him go into heaven". If these angels believe it and confess to Jesus very disciples can we do any less? Do we dare do less?

We could call many more witnesses to testify, but do we need more or are the ones we have already heard sufficient to win our case, and show our enemies His awesome Power? Knowing all of these things why don't we just shout out for all the world to hear, "THE JOY OF THE LORD IS MY

STRENGTH", and the mortal enemy of my soul cannot rob me of it.

WATCH FOR HE IS COMING

Being mere humans with all of our frailties and weaknesses, it is difficult for us to do all that God commands us to do and yet in the New Testament He through The Disciples tells us many times to "Watch and Pray", then later in Mark 13:33 It says "take heed, Watch and Pray; for ye know not when the time is". Mark 13:35 states "Watch ye therefore: for ye know not when the master of the house cometh, at even, or at midnight, or at the cockcrowing, or in the morning". Then in verse 37 it goes on to say, "And what I say unto all, "WATCH". Mark 14:37 states "Watch and pray lest ye enter into temptation. The Spirit truly is ready, but the flesh is weak". These Scriptures, and many more, too numerous to quote, however some of them are Mark 14:38, Matt 26:41, Acts 20:31, Eph 6:18, and 2Tim 4:5.

Don't be overwhelmed by the cares of this, after all if you have read the end of the book you know Jesus is coming again, and you must always be alert, and watch for we don't know the day or the time of His return. Studying the Scriptures gives us convincing proof that Jesus is coming again and we must be faithful to watch and pray at all times.

Unless we heed the word and let that word enter our hearts and the Holy Spirit quicken it, there will be very little, if any effect on us. This word warns us many times and in many ways that, "If any man have ears to hear let him hear" God has told us in the form of warning so many times, isn't it wonderful to realize that God loves us so dearly that He warns us not just once but many times. It is only if we know Jesus as our savior that we can hear the Holy Spirit open our hearts to the facts of His Second Coming.

How sad it is to think that at the time when He needed them the most, the Disciples He had chosen to go with Him in the

Garden of Gethsemane, let Him down in such a saddening way, they fell asleep after Jesus asked them to "Tarry Ye Here And Watch", while He went farther into the Garden to pray alone to His Father, His burden was for a world lost in sin and His prayers were so intense that He sweat drops of blood. This wasn't quite so bad as what they did later when He went back to them and found them sound asleep, after He woke them up and told them " Could you not watch one hour; watch ye and pray lest ye enter into temptation. The Spirit truly is willing but the flesh is weak". Then when He went back alone to pray and returned again later here they were fast asleep again, after awakening them He went back alone to pray, and then a third time He returned and found them sleeping. Just think of how this must have hurt Jesus, when He needed them in the worst way to pray for and support Him, here they were sleeping. Are we ever guilty of this, when we are needed by someone who is depending on us?

LIFES GUTTERS

Lord I dragged you through the gutters
Of this forsaken land
You never stopped your caring
Even kept me by your gentle hand

When I played the harlot though you won't look on sin
You still stood there beside me
Knocking on my hearts door asking to come back in
I heeded not your tear filled voice and went on my own way

The things I did oh Lord of mine
Are never pretty to recall
The sins that I had lived in
Were not a sudden fall

I started out oh so slowly
One small step at a time
Until I was ever closer
To that steepest of declines

Then I went hurtling downward
With a speed I could not stop
When I finally hit the bottom
There was no place to go but up

You still had your hand upon me
I heeded then your gentle call
You lifted me back to my starting point
Forgave each of my sins one and all

Showed what you had ahead for me
The souls for me to bring to you
The fields so ripe for harvest
Is where I fit into your plans

That you would use a wretch like me
Brings me humbly to bended knee
Make me worthy of your sweet love
Watch over me from heaven above

Your slightest wish is my command
I will travel over all this forsaken land
Bringing all the message of your love
Till you call me to my home above

Are we as Disciples of Christ doing the same thing those
Disciples did with him in the Garden, are we asleep as a world
that is lost has the heart of Christ yearning to have every soul
saved? There are lost souls in every country of the world that
grieve Jesus heart because they have not yet heard the good news
of Gods word, and the salvation of their souls through Jesus

Christ the savior of the world. How comfortable can we be living in the luxury we have while Jesus is hurting for them? I wonder if the very rocks will not cry out tears for these souls if we as Christians do not cry out for them instead of sleeping in our own comfort zones?

The Holy Ghost has warned us to "Take heed to yourselves lest at any time your hearts be overcharged with surfeiting, and drunkenness, and the cares of life, and so that day come upon you unawares". Rev 2:25 also warns us: "But that which ye have already, hold fast till I come". Hold fast to your faith and for the burden for lost souls, our spirit, soul, mind, and body, must be absolutely devoted to the Lord and His work here on this earth, we are His hands and feet here to do His work and His will in all things.

The parable of the sower in Luke 8:5-18 tells us that this seed which is spoken of is the word of God, and that there are four kinds of soil to plant this seed in. Of all the seed that was planted only one fell on good soil and brought forth fruit. This word of God planted into the soil is a good indication of the wonderful truth of Christ's returning for His saints Some hear the word but Satan comes and steals the word before it has the time to germinate and grow in their hearts, others hear this word, grasp it, have a wonderful blessing, then in a short while they become unburdened for others, cold hearted and just as indifferent as they were before the word came into their hearts. Then still another group hears the word, grasps it into their heart and then as they go back into the world the cares of this life, the deceit of riches, and pleasures of this world overcome this seed in their hearts and the fruit dies on the vine. But as was mentioned earlier there is the seed that falls into the good soil in a good heart and brings forth much fruit as they patiently nurture, fertilize, and water it with Gods word and the teaching of the Holy Spirit.

77

Charles (Chuck) A. De Land

SIGNS IN OUR WAITING TIME

When Jesus does come again will He find the Church full of faith, or will He find it dead as some are, full of much modernism, and no sign of the works of the Holy Spirit in some of them? We know that many churches are full of Gods Glory, and are doing His work and caring for His love, the souls of this lost and dieing world. We can give thanks for the ones who have taken His word and moved forward with it in faith and love, caring for others. Yet it is a sad fact that by comparison there are great masses, which have professed to be Christians, but because Modernistic Theology, Rationalism, Criticism, and Evolution are, sadly taking their toll on many Churches today and they do not worship God in Spirit and in truth.

GOD SEES

As you look down from heaven above
Do you glimpse the beauty of wondrous love
You created them all just for your pleasure
Then created man your love beyond measure

The gold the green the yellow hues
The red the amber the orange too
All attest to your awesome plan
And in it all you created man

Do you see my heart filled with love
As you gaze down from heaven above
Or is it black hard as stone
Not purest white with love alone

If it is black or hard as stone
Melt it Lord make it yours alone
Let it be filled with love divine
Be pure and white just as thine

There are many areas in this great nation where the Bible and belief in God and His word are being undermined, the philosophies of certain groups in these areas is devastating to the word of God. This shouldn't surprise us when we think that it has been this way throughout the history of the Church. There have been cults, and splinter groups that have set themselves against the teachings of Gods Word, and actually laughed at it, and then gone on in their own way as their thoughts led them. The faith of Christians, and the knowledge that what God has said will come true, and these same people who down grade, persecute, and ridicule true Christians will some day stand before God and be judged for their every act which is not covered by the blood of Jesus when He returns as He will. These lost ones have forgotten or disregarded the fact that Jesus will come again and that every knee will bow before Him and declare Him Lord of All.

We are living in the times of these doctrines of devils and seducing spirits, and we must be constantly on guard against them and make sure our hearts are open and pure before God so that we are not led astray by any of these teachings which are so crafty they make you think it might be alright to do some things which are actually against Gods will. We must be sure and test the Spirits before we make any move concerning spiritual matters.

Two thousand years ago Paul through the Holy Spirit wrote to Timothy in 2Tim 3:1-5, what sounds like history to us but was actually a prophecy. "This know also, that in the last days perilous times shall come, for men shall be lovers of their own selves, covetous, boasting, unthankful, unholy, without natural

79

affection, truce breakers, false accusers, incontinent, fierce, despisers of those that are good, traitors, heady, high minded, lovers of pleasures more than lovers of God; having a form of Godliness, but denying the power thereof: from such turn away".

Just look at the things that have happened in the recent past, homosexuals ply their deviations openly, our Presidents have illicit affairs, and still try to lead our country, students in schools shoot and kill fellow students, disgruntled employees walk into their work places and shoot fellow employees, and supervisors. Does this not sound as if Paul had been living in this present day, and telling us of these things after the fact, rather than two thousand years ago when he wrote them to Timothy?

As if he hadn't been right on the bulls eye with these predictions, look at what Matt., had to say, "For nation shall rise against nation, and kingdom against kingdom: and there shall be famines, pestilences, and earthquakes in divers places. All of these are the beginning of sorrows". Matt 14:7.

THE LIGHT

There is a light that sets men free
All who come will someday see
The peace and joy it brings to me
This precious light that sets souls free

That light is a rock standing firm
No shaking or trembling to cause alarm
That rock will hold us anchored strong
The savior will always walk along

There is a cross He bore alone
To show the lost a heavenly home
That light still shines for you and me
That all who come will be set free

How many time in the past seventy five years have nations gone to war with another over some slight, or pretext of insult: Have we had famines in many parts of the world, and do we today? Do we have diseases such as Aids running rampant throughout the world? What more needs to be said about this prophecy of Matthew? The entire world today is armed, ready to go to war with each other at any time. If we would only stop and realize that Gods plan is the return of Jesus to reign over all the earth and we will live in peace and for all eternity praising God and His Son.

In Daniel 12:4 we read very similar things; "The days are coming says the Sovereign Lord, when I will send a famine throughout the land, not a famine of food or a thirst for water, but a famine of hearing the word of the Lord. Men will stagger from sea to sea and wander from north to east, searching for the word of the Lord, but they will not find it", Could we possibly be living in these times right now? In spite of this Gods word still says to go into all the world and preach His word of love and salvation, regardless of the circumstances, if we are called to go and do this, right here at home or to the far flung reaches of the world.

It is imperative that we remember God said thousands of years ago that His chosen people, the Jews would return to their "Promised Land", and this came about in nineteen forty seven, when they once again became an independent nation. If this is not another sign of the return of Christ, then the entire Bible is false.

One more sign of the soon returning of Jesus is the fact stated in James 5:1-5, "Go to now, ye rich men, weep and howl for your miseries that shall come upon you. Your riches are corrupted; Your gold and silver is cankered; Ye have heaped treasure together for the last days". When you stop and think on this and then realize that ninety percent of the wealth of this nation is controlled by ten percent of the people, you must conclude that the amassing of these vast fortunes with the curses just mentioned is still another sure sign that our Lord is coming back soon, for things are all in place for His triumphant return.

WHAT OF SATAN

We are aware that Satan is the Prince of the power of the air and then in Eph. 6:12 we read that, "We wrestle not against flesh and blood, but against principalities, against powers, against the rulers of the darkness of this world". As if that isn't bad enough we have to contend with all of the sinners of this world, who belong to Satan and are helping him to persecute us in this warfare. This is why we must be ever vigilant and make prayer and fasting a part of our daily walk with the Lord, always remembering that God is always with you and that your victory has been purchased by the blood of Jesus.

At one time before we were saved and redeemed by Christ we belonged to Satan and lived in sin, but since we have been redeemed we now belong to God, and must let our light shine for Him in this world of sin, so that the light of Gods Gospel will illuminate the entire world, shining brightly for all to see. We must shine so brightly that those who have been blinded by the lies of Satan will have the scales removed from their eyes and see the truth of God's word and His love for them and all mankind. It is sad to think that those who do not see this light and receive it are blinded just as if they were in a cave where no light can penetrate and they are groping, trying to find the way out of the cavern they have taken themselves into by listening to Satan's lies, and plunging into his prison. If every Christian would let their light so shine before the world, that light would be so bright that Satan would have to leave because he cannot stand the light of God's truth, and would have to flee.

IF I DON'T

Father if I don't go and tell
This whole world will go to hell
Tell them how you sent your Son
That He would die to save each one

Am I a servant as Jesus said
How many to Him have I led
Do I love Him and others serve
Or do I sit and just observe

Go and tell all those you meet
Come and find your perfect peace
As you sit at the Saviors feet
Find true love and make your life complete

Don't say no as He calls your name
Then your life will not be the same
You will have peace as you speak His name
Your life will be forever changed

For our unsaved loved ones, and neighbors are just the same as those wandering around in that cavern, blindfolded by Satan, and walking around where the pitfalls and ledges could put them in extreme danger of dying in their sins. Jesus is life, and the light of the world and He will open the sin filled heart by His light. Who has the Holy Spirit spoken to you about lately and said, go and talk to that one and let them see Jesus love and compassion in you? Have you done it, or did you hold back fearing you might be rebuffed?

During the Tribulation period Satan will leave his headquarters in the air and come to earth and enter his center of power, but then at the end of that time, and then at the beginning of the Millenium an angel will come down from heaven who has a chain in one hand and the keys to the bottomless pit in the other. This angel will lay hold on Satan, bind him in chains, and cast him into that bottomless pit for one thousand years, put a seal on him so that he cannot deceive the nations of this world any more. However after the thousand years, Satan shall be released again to go out to deceive the nations which are in the four quarters of the earth, to come and do battle with and make war against Jesus, but he will be completely defeated, and then Satan and all of his, will be cast into the lake of fire for all of eternity.

GODS CURSE ON THE JEWISH NATION

The work of the Holy Spirit began at the birth of Jesus and will continue throughout the ages. The Holy Spirit is the representative of the Godhead here on earth. Since the Jews are a chosen people to God and until the crucifixion of Christ when they rejected Him they were highly favored, God gave them His word, He made many covenants with them giving them every opportunity for His continual blessings, but they rejected His love and care willingly, and would not recognize Jesus as the promised Messiah, being blinded by Satan's lies they were confused as to the first and second coming of Christ. Even though many Jews are coming to know Jesus as the Lord and savior, the nation as a whole are still living in darkness, and believing that the Messiah is still to come.

This is really sad when you think of all that God has done for them in the past, and has promised to do for them in the future, if they would only follow His plans and His direction for their lives. In spite of all their failures and shortcomings God still loves them, just as He still loves us in spite of our failures , He is ready and willing to forgive them if they will only open their eyes and hearts to receive Jesus as their Lord and Master. The blindness of the Jewish people will continue until the time of the Gentiles is fulfilled, and then at the close of the Tribulation, and the Millennium beginning , some of the Jews will see that Jesus is the Messiah and will mourn their rejection of Him for so many years, then they will turn to Him, repent for their sins and be saved.

JESUS PRAYER

Jesus prayed a prayer for me
That through the ages I might see
How each of us might join as one
Be as close as the Father and Son

He in us as we in Him
That our love would not grow dim
For the Father sent us His Son
That we might join those two as one

That we who God has given Him
Might be where He is and not grow dim
Our Father God in heaven above
Please let us always feel your love

Since you have given us to Him
He has called us each by name
This love that you have freely given
Will see us safely through to heaven

THE TIME OF THE GENTILES

When the Jewish people rejected Christ and He was crucified, God turned to the Gentiles and chose them to be the people of Jesus Kingdom. Jesus is the great King and His Kingdom will now be made up of both Jews and Gentiles because the Gentiles have been spliced into the vine, have believed, and have taken Gods word into all the world, and preached the Gospel to every creature, and are continuing to do so to this very day. What a wonderful promise we have from the Father when He says in Rev. 22:17, "And the Spirit and the bride say come. And let him that heareth say, come. And let him that is athirst come. And whosoever will, let him take the water of life freely". Praise the Lord this means that whosoever wills may come with a contrite and repentant heart and be saved.

This time will last until the Rapture and then the time as we know it will end. The Church today is a suffering Church for Christ, and are in a constant battle with the forces of evil, the world does not now, or does it ever want to understand Gods grace and forgiveness of sin. They would rather walk in darkness than in the light of Gods truth, and still God loves them and calls out to them through His Spirit. Jesus warned us that we must be constantly on guard for our souls because the world hates us because we are not of this world, so we must have on our full armor and, be in the battle, and on guard at all times for our own soul and the souls of the lost people of this world.

We still have this hope in us, that as we suffer now for Jesus we will also reign with Him in Glory, so the suffering we do now cannot compare to the glory that will be revealed in the fullness of time. The Church of Jesus Christ has always been a suffering Church when they have taken a stand for God's word and then stood firm on that Biblical stand. As soldiers in Gods Army we must be militant, self denying, sacrificing, and loyal to no one but God, with the courage to go forward into battle for Him when He gives the word. Some day soon the orders will come, soldiers of Jesus arise, go forward into the battle and know that the victory is ours. Jesus has loved us, cleansed us from sin with His own blood, and called us out from the world for a purpose.

Some day we will be kings and priests in Gods Kingdom, not in this life but in the Millennial age when we will reign with Jesus, if He is the one who is reigning in our hearts. Right now Satan is reigning in this evil world, and the saints of God are suffering. We must continue to keep our eyes and hearts on Jesus and fight on to the end. If we will only hold on we will inherit all of the things God has promised in His word.

CALVARY

I heard of a place called Calvary
Where Jesus died to set me free
Hung upon that cruel cross
The Angels mourned the earths great loss

Then I wondered why did He come
Knowing He would die on that tree
Only one reason why He left His throne
That He might die for a sinner like me

He took my place so I might live
Had but one priceless life to give
So I came to Him knelt at His feet
Thanks to Calvary my life is now complete

JESUS RETURNES

When the Rapture occurs we will be seized and secretly carried off by Jesus to the marriage supper of the Lamb. This Rapture will take place at the beginning of the Tribulation, and what a time that will be. In 2 Tim. 4:16 we read, "For the Lord Himself shall descend from heaven, and the dead in Christ shall be caught up together with them in the clouds to meet the Lord in the air, and so shall we ever be with the Lord". How wonderful to know that when we receive these glorified bodies and go forth with Jesus there will be no more sickness, pain, or suffering for eternity, as we meet Jesus in the air.

To put this into perspective take some pieces of glass, wood, dirt and pebbles in your right hand, then add some pins, needles, and nails, then in your left hand take a strong magnet. As you lower the magnet towards your right hand, the closer you get to the pins, needles, and nails they will rise, but not the glass, wood, dirt, and pebbles. Even though the pins, needles, and nails are covered by the dirt and other debris, they will still come to the magnet while the other things will simply remain in your hand. This is exactly what will happen in the Rapture of the Church, those whose hearts and lives are in complete harmony with Jesus will be attracted to Him and drawn up to meet Him in the air, but the ones who are not in complete harmony will stay in the gravity pull of this world.

We must keep our hearts pure, and our eyes upon Jesus at all times or we will not be attracted to Him when He steps out on that cloud and the trumpet sounds. As the metal objects were attracted to the magnet and the non-metal ones are not, this is what will happen, the pure in heart will arise but the unclean will remain in the dirt and mire of this world to repent, cry out, and possibly be martyred for their stand, if they are able to remain strong.

After the meeting of Jesus in the air there will be a time of rewards for those faithful ones who have followed Him here on earth. If He gives great rewards to those who have given a cup of cold water in His name, how much more will He give to those who have given their entire lives to His service? As humans we cannot possibly comprehend what it is that awaits us at this time, for every man will receive his own reward according to his labor, and every mans work will be revealed by fire, and if his works withstand the fire he will get his rewards. If any mans works are burned in the fire he will suffer loss, in other words our rewards will be diminished.

Every one who calls themselves a Christian has been called into a life of sacrifice, and self denial, God has given every one of us talents to be used for His glory, some are to preach, some to write, some to minister to the body, some to save souls by their witness, and so forth, all have been given some talent to use in the fields to labor for God. We must first seek the Kingdom of God, and put His interests and works first in our lives. It doesn't make any difference what our avocation might be, farmer, mechanic, business man, pastor or janitor, we have all been called into a life of self denial, and self sacrifice, we have been called to take up our cross daily, and follow Jesus wherever He leads us.

What about me, or you? Are we doing our best to save souls? Are we spending our time, money, and talents as He wants us to do? Will we be ashamed of our stewardship of what He has given us? Are we praying for lost souls? In short whatever we have, be it time, money, or talents, belongs to God and must be used wisely to further His Kingdom while we await His coming.

ANGELS SONG

Did you ever hear the angels sing
Have all your earthly fears take wing
What of a place called Golgotha Hill
Do you see the crosses standing still

Where Jesus died for you and me
That we could ever more be free
To come to Him through Gods Grace
Then someday look upon His face

Won't you come to Him right now
It's simple He will show you how
Throw your hearts door open wide
Let Jesus come and live inside

Forsake repent of all your sin
He will bring such joy within
Then as you live your sin free life
It will ever be free from strife

In Rev. 19: 6-9 we read a beautiful description of still another important event concerning the return of Christ, this is the Marriage Supper of the Lamb. These verses read as follows, "And I heard as it were the voice of a great multitude, and as the voice of many waters, and as the voice of mighty thunderings, saying, Alleluia: for the Lord God omnipotent reigneth: Let us be glad and rejoice, and give honor to Him: for the marriage of the Lamb is come, and His wife hath made herself ready. And to her that was granted that she should be arrayed in fine linen, clean and white: for the fine linen is the righteousness of saints. And He told me write, Blessed are they which are called unto the Marriage Supper of the Lamb. And He saith unto me, these are the true sayings of God."

When we become Christians and start serving our Lord it is our duty and responsibility to go out and influence others for Christ, and they in turn are to go forth and influence still others until the time of the return of our Lord, and the rapture of His Church. If Jesus were to return today would He find you ready and working while you are awaiting His return, or would He find you getting cozy with the world and living close to the sins of the world, if not actually committing their sins?

THE TRIBULATION

This is a time of great trial and testing, it goes from the Rapture of the Church, through Tribulation. The Church which has been caught up to meet Christ in the air will miss this Tribulation. The Tribulation will be the absolute darkest period in the history of the world, and the antichrist will be enjoying his full power. It is not only possible, but highly probable that many during this period will humble themselves and get saved, and for this they will receive instant death. The antichrist will not stand for anyone to worship God, he wants complete servitude and allegiance to him and him alone.

Matt. 24:21-22 tells us of this Tribulation, "For then shall be great tribulation, such as was not since the beginning of the world to this time, no, nor shall be. And except those days be shortened, there should no flesh be saved: but for the elects sake those days shall be shortened".

Then in Rev. 3:10 we read, "Because thou hast kept the word of my patience, I will also keep thee from the hour of temptation, which shall come upon all the world, to try them that dwell upon the earth". Then again in Rev. 14: 6-7 it says, " And I saw another angel fly in the midst of heaven, having the everlasting Gospel to preach unto them that dwell on the earth, and to every nation, and kindred, and tongue, and people, saying with a loud voice, fear God and give glory to Him; for the hour of His judgement is come: and worship Him".

In other words every person on earth who is not taken in the rapture will be forced to make a choice. This choice will be to either accept Jesus Christ as Lord and saviour of their lives, and be martyred by the antichrist, or to accept him as their master, receive his mark, and then bring upon themselves the eternal wrath of God. Again in Rev. 14: 9-10, we read more about this, it says, "If any man worship the beast and his image, and receive his mark, the same shall drink of the wrath of God, and he shall be tormented with fire and brimstone". The choice is obvious for any one who knows the least little bit about God, His Son Jesus Christ, and the things God has stated in His word. Be ready for the Rapture, I beg you.

Who the antichrist will be doesn't make a bit of difference to the Christian who is living a holy life for God. The most important thing for us to remember is that we must be ready to go up with Jesus when He steps out on the cloud and calls His Bride home, Let us be about the business of winning souls for the Christ, as we go through every day from the time we awaken until we go to bed at night, planting the seeds of salvation, watering the seeds others have planted, or reaping the harvest for Gods Glory, when the harvest time comes.

We do know that in Rev.20:4, that God will richly reward those who are martyred, it states, " And I saw thrones, and they sat upon them, and judgment was given unto them: and I saw the souls of them that were beheaded for the witness of Jesus, and for the Word of God, and which had not worshipped the beast, neither his image, neither had received his mark upon their foreheads, or in their hands, and they lived and reigned with Christ a thousand years".

Rev. 20:1-3 tells us that as the millennium begins an angel will come down from heaven having the key to the bottomless pet, and a chain in his hand and will lay hold on the dragon, who is satan, bind him for a thousand years, and cast him into the bottomless pit, seal him and stop him from deceiving the nations for a thousand years.

THE MILLENNIUM PERIOD

The millennium period will begin when Jesus closes the Tribulation period and starts the millennium. At this time the saints will have even greater glories ahead of them than they have already experienced. Please, you who know Jesus Christ as Lord cling to His Cross, endure the trials and shame the world will heap upon you, and suffer as you must for His Glory. Then I must plead with you who do not know Him as your Lord and saviour, please ask Him to forgive your sins, come into your hearts, and purify you for eternity. It is better to suffer now and then reign with Jesus in glory than to reject Him, have your own way in the world, and then suffer in hell for eternity.

One of the first things that will happen in this new age will be the judgment of the living nations. This will occur separately from the "Great White Throne Judgment", because this Judgment is reserved for sinners as individuals. This Judgment on the nations will be very severe for those who have had a great light and not walked in it, I hate to dwell on the fate of this great nation we live in if our people do not humble themselves, turn from their wicked ways, and call upon the Lord and ask forgiveness of their sins.

THE SAVIOR

What a savior you are to me
You love me forgave me set me free
For you said to the Father
Let me be that final lamb

All you sinners please come to me
I alone can set your soul free
Do not delay come as you are
Only my love can draw from afar

Then I will never leave you
I will carry you through every trial
For in the end you will be so very happy
And once again your heart can smile

So come to me all of you sinners
Enjoy my blessed and perfect peace
For I alone can ever forgive you
That your soul will have my release

All of God's creation will be groaning for deliverance at this time, and deliverance will only come when we have the glorious reign of Jesus with all of His saints. Rev. 11:15, tells us about this, "and the seventh angel sounded; and there were great voices in heaven, saying, the kingdoms of this world are become the kingdoms of our Lord, and of His Christ; and He shall reign forever and ever". Jesus will be enthroned as, "King of Kings and Lord of Lords", He will share His awesome glory and honor with us and we will then have the honor bestowed on us by our blessed savior. Jesus promises that, "To him that overcometh will I grant to sit with me in my throne".

Our finite minds cannot possibly comprehend the great and glorious reign of Jesus. These things will not only affect mankind, but every part of Gods creation. We know that satan will be bound for one thousand years and that though his power now is great, because he uses all of the unsaved people as his agents here on earth to work his havoc on the world, but when he is cast into the bottomless pit this power is entirely lost.

The present world governments will be eliminated, no more United Nations, European Common Market, kingdoms, dictatorships, democracies, or any other kind, except for Gods plans which are so much better than mans, that there can be no comparison made. We will be governed by God Himself, and this will be a great government. We don't know exactly what it will be since there are no details listed in His word. From what we can glean from the word in many places in the Word of God, Jesus will use His saints to aid Him in many ways to carry out His governing over cities, states, and nations. We have no way of knowing who will rule where, however we do know that Jesus will appoint who He will to rule over each area, and He will be the ultimate judge and Lord of all.

This leadership also includes the animal world, which will no longer eat flesh as they now do, the wolf will dwell with the lamb, the leopard with the kid: the calf and the young lion will eat together, and a little child shall lead them. Isaiah 11:6-9 goes on to state, "The cow and the bear shall feed: and their young ones shall lie down together: and the lion shall eat straw like the ox. And the suckling child shall play on the hole of the asp, and the weaned child shall put his hand on the cockatrice den. They shall not hurt nor destroy in all my holy mountain: for the earth shall be full of the knowledge of the Lord as the waters cover the seas:

What a change for the better this will be, the animal world will be as they were in Noah's day on the Ark, no more warfare amongst them, only the complete peace of God manifested amongst the animal in their relationships with one another and with mankind.

There will be no more wars among men, and the peace of God shall reign, Isaiah 2:4, tells us that, "and they shall beat their swords into plowshares, and their spears into pruning hooks: Nation shall not lift up sword against nation, neither shall they learn war any more". When you read this you know that the only hope for peace in this world is the coming of Jesus. While nations are talking about peace, we have wars, and unrest throughout the earth, with millions of soldiers under arms, and each nation trying to get the advantage over all of the others, with arms, and nuclear weapons, biological weapons, and the fear of many clandestine methods of reprisal, terrorism among them.

However when Jesus returns evil will be restrained, satan will be in the bottomless pit and Jesus with His saints will be ruling the earth. Yet when satan is released for a little season he will gather together immense armies to again make war. The ones who join him will be those who were outwardly good because they were under such a powerful restraint from Jesus and His saints, yet when satan returns and beguiles them they will drop their restraint and go back into their sin. Even though it had been a time of Holiness with Jesus reigning with a rod of iron, sin will remain in the hearts of many until satan is released from the bottomless pit. Sin will only be completely destroyed on earth at the time of the final renewing of the age. Whatever you do if you have the least desire to know about this last final renewing, be certain that your heart is with God and His Son, and then you will be there to experience it all for yourself.

THE LITTLE SEASON OF SATAN

One thousand years in the bottomless pit has not changed satan in the least, he still hates Jesus and His saints, and everything righteous that they stand for. After he is released satan will go about gathering together the greatest armies of history and then he will make one last attempt to defeat God's plans, but he will be absolutely and completely defeated.

The little season is summed up in Rev. 20:7-10, "And when the thousand years are expired, satan shall be loosed out of his prison, and shall go out to deceive the nations which are in the four quarters of the earth. Gog and Magog, to gather them together to battle: the number of whom is as the sand of the sea. And went up on the breadth of the earth, and compassed the camp of the saints about, and the beloved city: and fire came down from God out of heaven, and devoured them. And the devil that deceived them was cast into the lake of fire and brimstone, where the beast and the false prophet are, and shall be tormented day and night for ever and ever".

It is very obvious from this that satan has made his last and final attack in his desperation, and has lost, his final assault against Jesus and His saints has resulted in his complete and absolute defeat. Jesus heel was bruised as is stated, but Jesus has bruised the head of satan, and thus sealed his doom for ever and ever.

THE GREAT WHITE THRONE JUDGEMENT

Rev. 20: 11-15 describes this event in every detail, showing that God sits on His throne and judges the dead, both small and great, and that the books were opened: then another book was opened which is called, "The Book of Life", and the dead are judged out of the things which are written in this book, according to their works, also the seas give up the dead which are in them. Then hell delivers the dead which are in there, and they are judged every man according to his works, and death and hell are cast into the lake of fire.

PRAYERS

Jesus heard my prayer today
For I heard His Spirit say
I hear my child you are blessed
What I will do is for the best

As I hear oh Lord of mine
Let me always do your will divine
Hear you speak to me each day
Follow every word I hear you say

Show me one to comfort just now
Then oh Lord please show me how
Let my heart be filled with love
Sent by you from heaven above

Then Lord at the end of day
Let me hear your Spirit say
Well done my child take your rest
Knowing my heart you have blessed

If these events don't drive Gods people to their knees to intercede for the lost souls of this world, and break their hearts with the burden God has put there, then we should fall on our knees in repentance, and ask God to forgive us for having such a hardened heart. We need to feel the burden for these poor lost souls wherever we see them, or even think about them, in such a way that when they see us they will know that we feel a deep burden, and longing, for them to come to know Jesus as their saviour.

It is so easy to pass by a lost soul without even thinking of them or where they are headed if we don't soften our hearts and reach out to them in Gods love and compassion, We must ask ourselves every day, am I doing everything that I can for the salvation of my loved ones, for my neighbors, and above all my enemies? For all of the lost scattered across this world? Now is the time, while there is still time, to search our own souls and go forth searching for those who are lost, with only us as their hope to help them away from that terrible lake of fire and brimstone for all of eternity.

EVERYTHING NEW FOR ETERNITY

We can never leave the lost in this life, and we must never forget to pray for them as long as we live, however when we enter the New Heaven and the New Earth stages of the future we will see what the glory of our eternal home is and not just the glimpses we get about it in the Bible. We know that with our human minds we could never grasp the things that God has in store for us when we get there.

We know form Rev. 21:1 that there will be a New Heaven, and a New Earth, and that the first heaven and first earth will be passed away and there will be no more sea. This is in itself hard for us to comprehend, and yet since it is part and parcel of the Word of God we know that it will come to pass, and that we will be a part of the New Heaven and the New Earth.

In Rev. 21:9-11, John describes the New Jerusalem descending out of heaven from God, and having Gods glory, with her light like a jasper stone, clear as crystal, and she has no need of the sun, or the moon to shine in it: for the glory of God will light it and the Lamb is the light thereof.

In Rev. 22:1-2, we read, " And He showed me a pure river of water of life, clear as crystal, and proceeding out of the throne of God and of the Lamb. In the midst of the street of it and on either side of the river, was there the tree of life, which bare twelve manner of fruits, and yielded her fruit every month: and the leaves of the trees were for the healing of the nations". In addition to this we find that God will make His tabernacle with men, and dwell with them, in the same manner He did with Adam, and the people will belong to God. He will wipe away all tears from their eyes, and there will be no more death, or sorrow, or pain. What a wonderful glimpse of what we have to look forward to, seeing God, Jesus, the Holy Spirit, Apostles, family

Charles (Chuck) A. De Land

and friends to see and to talk with, worship God and His Son, and in general see and enjoy the things God has reserved for us.

RELY ON HIM

Are you perplexed want to scream
Everything has gone wrong it seems
Just throw yourself in Jesus arms
He will always calm your fieriest storms

Lean on Him He will not fail
All of your problems will quickly pale
So call on him and His great love
He will hear from heaven above

His presence always brings such peace
Your troubles He will give release
He will hear your every cry
On Him alone you must rely

I would be remiss if I didn't stop and ask myself and those who read these words a few questions relating to Jesus and His second coming. Then I want to close with a final scripture, Rev. 22:20-21, after the questions.

1. Do I enjoy being a Christian, praying, reading the Bible?

2. Does my heart desire a closer walk with the Lord at all times; Do I enjoy being alone and communing with Him?

3. Do I lift up Jesus wherever I am and whatever I am doing; Is Jesus life reproduced in me?

4. Do I do good to others wherever the opportunity presents itself?

104

5. Am I truly helping others who are depressed or burdened, caring about them, praying with them?

6. Am I crucified with Jesus every day?

7. Do I constantly seek those things which are above?

8. Do I keep my body in complete subjection to the will of God and the guidance of the Holy Spirit?

9. Do I keep my words sweet and pure, always guarding my tongue and lips?

10. Am I a faithful steward of the things God has blessed me with, my time, my talents, my finances?

11. Do I tithe faithfully, or sacrifice so that I have more to give, not only to God but to those less fortunate?

12. If Jesus should come today would I welcome Him or would I be fearful?

Enough questions, I'm sure these will give you room for some soul searching, now for Rev. 22: 20-22. "Surely I come quickly: Amen. Even so, come Lord Jesus. The grace of our Lord Jesus Christ be with you all. "Amen".

THE END

HEAVENS GATE

What of the bars of heavens gate
They warn all sinners of their fate
They have chosen a life of sin
At heavens portals they cannot go in

So when you stand before that gate
Will you have to stand and wait
Or will it swing and open wide
That you may freely walk inside

If your life is free of any sin
And you indeed can enter in
What glory will you then perceive
The human mind cannot conceive

With beauty love and praising God
By all the saints who praise the Lord
Those bars across the heavenly gate
Will only seal a sinners fate

ABOUT THE AUTHOR

I was fifty-five years of age in 1981 when I accepted Jesus Christ as my Lord and Savior, and He immediately renewed my love for writing and for poetry. I first started writing poetry when I was in the second or third grade in school, and continued until I was married, then it seemed to be forgotten until I came to know the Lord.

Since that time God has reestablished my talent to write not only poetry, but short articles in order to glorify Him, knowing full well it is not my ability, but a gift from God to be used for Him, and by Him as He touches those who read them.

May God bless all those who read these words is my fervent prayer.